James McCosh

Syllabus of Lectures on Philosophy

James McCosh

Syllabus of Lectures on Philosophy

ISBN/EAN: 9783337239152

Printed in Europe, USA, Canada, Australia, Japan

Cover: Foto ©Thomas Meinert / pixelio.de

More available books at **www.hansebooks.com**

PREFACE.

The Class of '79 was the first to issue printed Notes in this department. It was immediately seen that they supplied a want long felt. Of all things, accuracy of expression is most desired when dealing with philosophic opinions. In the bustle of the class-room this desideratum is often lost, and the only remedy is a well prepared set of printed Notes. Last year copies were procured only with the greatest difficulty and at the highest expense; hence the new issue.

The first part of the Notes has been to a great extent rewritten; re-arrangement and explanatory remarks have been added to the latter half.

It is, therefore, hoped that the Notes have been improved and rendered more accurate.

PRINCETON, N. J., September, 1882.

INDEX.

HISTORY OF PHILOSOPHY.

INTRODUCTION.

What is Philosophy? Ueberweg calls it the Science of Principles.

Dr. Adam Smith shows us the fact that in rude societies there is little or no desire, and certainly no opportunity, for science and speculation. Division of labor has acted as important a part in the advancement of science as of national wealth. If the same individual has to make his own clothing, to be his own shoemaker, his own baker, his own blacksmith, etc., he will not excel in any one branch of industry—his attention being directed over so extensive a field.

As civilization sets in, there is a wider and wider division of labor. Thus, for example, take the manufacture of a pin: One man draws out the wire, another cuts it in due lengths, a third draws out the point, a fourth files and fits the top to receive the head; while the making of the head is another operation—the fastening, another still; and whitening the whole, is a separate process, employing as many more. So, in the manufacture of a single pin, eighteen distinct operations have to be gone through with. Now, if a single man were to perform all these, he could make, perhaps, from one to twenty a day; whereas, by the present process, there are made at least 4500.

It was thought strange by some, that such a man as Dr. Smith, who was an extremely discerning writer, should introduce a work with such an apparently unimportant subject. But his sagacity led him to see that division of labor lies at the foundation of civilization.

Bacon remarks, and justly, that "he who will not work, ought not to eat." Science is as much a work as agriculture, for, in order to knowledge and refinement, some must think, while others follow a handicraft. Thought is, moreover, a necessity of our being, and in the intervals of early pastoral labors it was ever curious and busy. The shepherds of old, while guarding their flocks by night, must gaze upon the blue dome above them, and be led to seek to penetrate into its mysteries. Isaac, when he went out at eventide, found a vast number of questions resting upon his mind, and, eager to solve them, his mind quickened under the strain, and bounded into fresh activity. In early times men had an immense number of topics to resolve. They must think of all subjects, for all are unknown. When the sage of old surveyed the stars, there was no Newton to unlock for him the mysterious influence by which planet after planet circled in space. When he gazed upon the earth there was no geologist to interpret to him the handwriting of Nature in her strata. He must try to grasp all these and resolve them at once—of course, without success. There may have occasionally been one whose native taste led him to bestow his attention on one branch in preference to another; but generally, in early ages we see science attempting everything, and exhausting nothing.

Science was then not classified, because unknown.

At first, theology, metaphysics, and physics, and other sciences were blended together, and then they came to be treated apart. Speculations of the former kind were common to the dwellers on the banks of the Euphrates, Ganges, and Nile. Philosophy is full of it. Theosophy is a good name for it; and speculators of this kind were called sophists, or sages.

Let us put ourselves in the position of a sage on the banks of the Nile. He is compelled by an irresistible impulse of his nature to investigate, speculate, etc. A modern would betake himself to experiment, perhaps a rigid analysis with his chemical retort. But this man has no scientific instruments, no algebra or geometry to apply. How is he to investigate? Can he make a retort? He does not even know its value. He is compelled to resort to speculation. Thus we see that a necessity is created, as society advances, for the division of intellectual as well as manual labor. This was recognized at an early date, and gave rise to rival schools, with rival theories.

In Greece the first division of the sciences was made. The Eleatics, who flourished 550 B. C. and with whom metaphysical speculation is supposed to have originated, adapted themselves to metaphysical speculations, and sought to penetrate the mystery of being. The Pythagorean school confined itself to numbers and forms; the Ionic to physics. Thus things began to be divided. Plato again mixed metaphysics along with all other topics, under the name of Dialectics. His great treatise is the "Timæus:" it discussed the nature of God, of man, and treated of the physical sciences; it was, in fact, an encyclopædia of knowledge. Plato discovers everything essentially Greek. Aristotle better anticipated modern science.

The *Eleatic School*, as we have said, was founded and adapted itself to metaphysical speculations. The *Pythagorean* endeavored to reduce all things to the fundamental principles of proportion and harmony. Then there was the *Atomic School*, of Lucippus and Democritus, and Anaxagoras with his *ὁμοιομέρειαι*.

The division of intellectual labor appeared first in the Pan-Hellenic confederacy. We have first the *Ionic* school of Thales, dealing with the elements: secondly, the *Pythagorean*, dealing with numbers and forms; and, thirdly, the *Eleatic*, dealing with being.

In Plato everything is discussed—the elements of all things—eternal and fixed parts are distinguished from mutable things—the stars going west, etc.; in short, he was a complete cosmologist. Aristotle was the medium between the sage and the modern philosopher. The division of intellectual labor was accomplished more particularly by Bacon. It is a common saying that Nature produces a great man once in a century. It produces a Bacon, however, but once in a thousand years.

In consequence of the division of labor in science attempts have been made to classify the sciences. An old classification was:

1. What things are.
2. What things ought to be.

3. How truths are to be discussed.

Bacon classified them in accordance with the faculties employed:

1. History, from the memory.
2. Poetry, from the imagination.
3. Philosophy, from the reason.

One of the best classifications of the physical sciences is that given by Comte, a man of idiosyncracies, but of profound ability, and founder of the Positive system of Philosophy.

His classification is of the physical sciences alone, for the mental he classes under these. It is superior to Bacon's, for it gives the reason for his division, which is, that those sciences to be first investigated should be the simplest, and their laws most readily discovered and applied. From these he proceeds as from the principles to the more complex. (See Atwater's Logic, pp. 218–221.) This classification explains the progress of the different sciences, and how each is dependent upon the other.

Thus the most simple idea is space, therefore Geometry was the first to attain perfection. Then came its application to objects; first to the unorganized—the simpler—and among these the heavenly bodies; hence arose Astronomy. Then came Natural Philosophy, or Terrestrial Physics, in studying which we may take two methods; the simple or mechanical, and the chemical, which only came in in 1790. After these came the study of Organic and Social Physics. Comte also had another famous generalization. He said all sciences are: 1. Theological, 2. Metaphysical, and 3. Positive. In this Comte erred, because he has driven into a corner many equally important sciences, for, being a materialist, he omitted the mental sciences, treating them under Physiology.

We must, however, study the mind, which studies other things, for we cannot examine the spiritual world by means of the senses. Yet the study of the mind comes later, for men look out of themselves before they look in. There is, however, a progression which we shall be able to trace. The Ionic and Italic (Pythagorean) schools lay down two opposing schemes. How shall we determine between them? This must be done by the aid of dialectics. Hence Logic,

Minerva-like, sprang full-armed from the brain of Aristotle. By it these studies were more readily carried on. He produced his system before there was any physical science.

In Aristotle's time there were already metaphysical (in its broad sense) sciences. Ethics, the science of right and wrong, was already established by Socrates. This was scientifically done, with the intent to distinguish between natural ethics and ethics as given by God. But, say sceptics, may not ethics and logic be a delusion? Hence arises metaphysics. The father of this in modern times was Descartes, followed by Leibnitz, Kant, Jacobi, Shelley, and Hegel.

The examination of the mind began in ancient times with Aristotle, in later times with Locke. This is a field to be closely pursued, as it will settle the disputed points in Metaphysics, which "mingle their waters."

Aristotle founded Rhetoric, Philosophy, Natural History, Psychology, and Logic. Mathematics was already brought to a high state of perfection.

We owe induction to Bacon; not that no man had applied it to any extent before, but because he first made it the subject of examination, and set men upon the scientific pursuit of it. As a result we have modern Physics, and all its practical inventions.

We have, therefore, first the undeveloped sciences, then the sciences as developed, then the mixed. These are shown below.

1. Undeveloped Sciences.

2. Developing Sciences.
   - Material Sciences.
     - Mathematics.
     - Astronomy.
     - Terrestrial Physics.
     - Chemistry.
     - Physiology.
     - Geology.
       - Compte also brings in Social and Individual Physics.
   - Mental Sciences.
     - Psychology. (Aristotle, founder.)
     - Logic. (Aristotle, founder.)
     - Ethics. (Socrates, founder.)
     - Kalology. (Plato, founder.)
     - Metaphysics. (Appeared first.)

3. Mixed Sciences. { Natural Theology. / Social Sciences. / Philology. / Political Science.

We are to treat chronologically and historically of the mental sciences.

Philosophy seems to have made its first appearance in the East in the ancient lands of Chaldea, of Egypt, and, perhaps, of India. In the latter country philosophy is inseparably mixed with theology, and, consequently, there are but occasional guesses at physical phenomena. Their system, if system it was, might rather be called a theosophy than a philosophy. Inquiries into the nature of God is the prevailing character of all eastern theosophy; and the first indication of philosophy is a separation of these inquiries, and their philosophy proper begins to take its place.

Here we have to distinguish between spontaneous and reflective thought.

The first is common to all men.

Reflective thought is that which distinguishes man from man. It bends back and examines spontaneous thought. It began through necessity about 700–500 B. C. Men began to enquire for the τέλος. It appears in Confucius of China 550 B. C. He applied it to morals, and with him morality took the form of a law.

His system was independent of religion; that is, he dedevoted himself to worldly affairs; duty or immortality is not once mentioned in his system. About the same time rose a certain set of philosophers who made inquiries into the nature of God. This is briefly the character of the early philosophy. Shortly after these, Buddhism arose; a system of mysticism ending in atheism. At the same time there appeared a similar system in Persia; two principles, good and evil, in eternal conflict. The Hebrews were of earlier date—Solomon and the prophets about the same time as those in Greece, 600–700 B. C.

Deeper inquiries now began to be made. Such questions were asked as, "What is wisdom?" "What is the course and origin of nature?" By the senses we have some knowledge of things around us; but through them, what knowledge can we have of wisdom? Such investigations

Sect II

Spontaneous thought is essentially [illegible]
[illegible]
[illegible]
[illegible]
[illegible]
[illegible] philosophy [illegible]
human [illegible]
[illegible] [illegible] [illegible] [illegible] [illegible]
[illegible]
[illegible]
[illegible]
[illegible]
[illegible]
[illegible]

[illegible]
[illegible]

were instituted (500, 600 B. C.) by the Greek-speaking people of Asia Minor. Not that they were the first to put such questions; for we find in the Book of Proverbs the inquiry: "What is wisdom?" Men are not satisfied simply with knowledge gained by the senses. There are other faculties craving knowledge. The Jew pointed to God as the embodiment of knowledge and the source of wisdom. But their books do not profess to be a philosohy, but only to reveal the will of God in regard to man's destiny.

Philosophy, then, may be said to have had its rise among the Greeks of Asia. It is very difficult, however, to determine how far these early philosophers may have drawn from eastern theosophy. Certain philosophers arose around Miletus and Ephesus, towns intimately connected with eastern countries. But what the Greek drew from others he speedily made his own, and left upon it the imprint of his genius.

Their statuary and painting came originally from the Egyptians, but under their skill their works far surpassed the ungraceful models from Egypt.

It was so, likewise, in poetry. Homer and Hesiod were not, probably, independent of the ballads of the East; for it seems impossible that such perfect productions should have been written without suggestions from other sources. They derived some, at least, from eastern countries; but still they gave their own character to their productions.

There are no very accurate means of knowing anything about the history and theories of these early philosophers. They did not commit their doctrines to writing, but gathered a few disciples around them and taught orally. The several sources are:

1. The Dialogues of Plato.
2. The Philosophic Works of Aristotle. These two are the most reliable.
3. Diogenes Laertius, 200 or 300 B. C.
4. The Commentators on Aristotle.
5. The Works of Plutarch, (Pseudo.)
6. Plautus and the Neo-Platonists.

7. The Christian Fathers; who often quoted from the philosophic writers, their object being to explain the Scriptures.

8. Cicero.

In addition to these a few fragments have come down to us; in particular, from the writings of Xenophanes and Parmenides and a fragment of a Sicilian philosophical poem. From these sources we learn something of their doctrines.

Greek philosophy, then, begins about 600 B. C. It has three marked forms with distinct features:

THE FIRST PERIOD OF PHILOSOPHY is divided into three parts:

I. Pre-Socratic.—Scattered schools.
   There were three parties in the Pre-Socratic school, speculative, independent, and original.

II. Combined transitory state; under Socrates, Plato, Aristotle.

III. The Post-Aristotelian philosophy (to the Platonic inclusive). A cosmopolitan, Athenian philosophy spreading over the whole world. Academy, Perepatetics, Stoics, Epicureans, called Disciplinæ.

I (a) Jones B. [illegible]
(c) [illegible]

Intermediate [illegible]
[illegible] Horace
These should [illegible]

G[illegible] [illegible] [illegible]
its [illegible]

CHAPTER I.

PERIOD I.—ANCIENT PHILOSOPHY.

PRE-SOCRATIC SCHOOLS.

IONIC.	PYTHAGOREAN.	ELEATIC.
Key Note, στοιχεῖα, "Elements."	Key Note, "Numbers and Form."	Key Note, τὸ ὄν, Being.
Thales, "Water." Born 35th Olympiad.	Pythagoras, Born 49th Olympiad.	Xenophanes, Born 60th Olympiad.
Anaximander, "τὸ ἄπειρον," Born 42d Olympiad	Archytas, "Musical System." B. C. 504–460.	Parmenides, Born 65th Olympiad.
Anaximenes, "Air," (see below.) Died 63d Olympiad.	Philolaus.	Zeno, Born 70th or 71st Olympiad.
Diogenes, "The Warm Air." Born 80th Olympiad.		Melissus, Born 82d or 84th Olympiad.

I.—PRE-SOCRATIC PHILOSOPHY.

The Greeks easily noticed the difference between night and day, then between the seasons: thus Astronomy arose, with the ability to determine eclipses of the sun and moon. Thought went beyond the φαινόμενα to the real. Hence the universal tendency of the Pre-Socratic Philosophy was to find a principle to explain nature. Nature is the most immediate, that which first meets the eye. It is the most palpable, that which first arouses the enquiring mind. At the basis of its changing forms, beneath its manifold appearances they thought there lay a first principle which remained the same through all changes. The question thus arose, what is the "ἀρχή"? (a phrase used by Anaximander)—what is the origin of things? The answers were three in number, marking three different schools.

A.—The Ionic School.

Inquiry.—*Περὶ φύσεως*; how things originate; their essential nature; their ἀρχή.

Method.—Analytic and empirical, not inductive; proceeded immediately from the observation of a few facts to general laws.

Doctrine.—To solve the problem as to the ἀρχή of all things, we must seek for some element, *στοιχεῖον*. The ἀρχή was the primordial something endowed with motive and transmutative force, so as to generate all the variety of products, each successive and transient, which our senses witness. It was found in water, chaotic matter (ἄπειρον) and air.

Tendency.—Pantheistic, did not distinguish between God and His works.

1. Thales, (640–548 B. C.) contemporary with Solon and Crœsus. A citizen of Miletus, born in the 35th Olympiad, of Phœnician origin, which seems to be a clear proof of the connection between Eastern and Greek philosophy. It is thought that Moscus, said to have been Moses, was his teacher; sometimes, indeed, he is confounded with Moses. He traveled in Egypt and astonished the people by measuring the heights of the pyramids by their shadows. According to him the ἀρχή, or "principle of all things," is *water*. "From water and into water everything returns." Let us now look into his feelings and endeavor to find out how he came to adopt this principle. He saw that everything changed from what it originally was. Now he seeks to penetrate beyond and beneath the mere phenomena of change and find out the cause. It has been stated by Aristotle that he said that all things are nourished by water. Now Thales, perceiving that dampness belonged to the seed

and nourishment of things, that warmth is developed from moisture, and that all things are preserved by water, therefore argues generally that water must be the ἀρχή—*the plastic living and life-giving principle.*

The philosophical significance of Thales does not appear to have extended further than the first principle. Subsequent narrators, however, relate that he set up the idea of a world soul—some living power in the universe. Plato, in *De Cœlo*, says that he maintained that amber and magnet possessed a living soul, because they were possessed of a moving power. He is included among the seven sages of Greece. He wrote no books. It is reported of him that he was the first to calculate an eclipse. (See Herodotus.) His doctrine is dynamical, not mechanical; its tendency is pantheistic.

He believed in God, but did not separate God and His works, and held that God was in all things. Those who held these views were called Physiologists. (περὶ φύσεως.)

2. Anaximander, (611–540 B. C.) Also a native of Miletus. He is represented as the companion of Thales. The first to lay aside the defective mode of oral tradition and to commit the principles of natural science to writing. Mathematics and astronomy were greatly indebted to him. He was the first to delineate the surface of the earth and mark the divisions of land and water upon a brazen plate. The invention of the sun-dial is also mistakenly ascribed to him. Said to have been the first to calculate the size and distances of the heavenly bodies. The first to call the essential essence of all things ἀρχή. Committed his teaching to poetic writing, but they have not been preserved. This principle he defined as the "unlimited, eternal and unconditioned;" as that which embraced and ruled all things, and which, since it lay at the basis of all determinateness of the finite and the changeable, is itself infinite and indeterminate. He held that τὸ ἄπειρον, (rude space), the limitless, infinite, is the first principle in all things; that the universe, though variable in its parts, as one whole is immutable: and that all things are produced from infinity and terminate in it. What this philosopher meant by "infinity" has been a subject of much controversy. If we follow the testimony of Aristotle and Theophrastus, it appears to be only a mere

philosophical expression for the same thought which the old cosmogonists have attempted to utter in their representation of chaos—τὸ μῖγμα—a mixture of multifarious elementary parts out of which individual things issued by separation. Out of this chaos, τὸ ἄπειρον, arose thus the infinite—a something intermediate between air and water—giving order and form.

This ἀρχή includes the fundamental contraries, hot, cold, moist, dry, in a potential or latent state; including further a self-developing and self-changing force, and being immortal and indestructible. From these contraries all elements are evolved. He thought the globe was originally made of earth and moisture. By the heat of the sun, a blazing wheel, the moisture was dried up and left earth; but during the process living creatures arose from the fermenting bubbles, first in the form of fishes, and then assumed higher forms.

Here we have an anticipation of modern theories, especially a dim view of the La Place theory.

3. Anaximenes, (557–500 B. C.) Also of Miletus. Is called by some "the scholar;" by others, the companion of Anaximander; but there is a resemblance between his doctrines and those of Thales. He made *air* the principle of all things. But by *air* and *water* we must not understand chemical air and water. Water meant a liquid state: the air, a subtile ether animated with a divine principle whence it becomes the origin of all beings. He held air to be God, because it is diffused through all nature and is perpetually active. Perceiving that air surrounds the whole world, that breath conditions the activity of life, and that the soul rules us, he seems to have been led to take this position. He is said to have taught, therefore, that all minds are air; that fire, water, and earth proceed from it by rarefaction or condensation; that the sun and moon are fiery bodies, whose form is that of a circular plate; that the stars, which also are fiery substances, are fixed in the heavens as nails in a crystalline plane; and that the earth is a plane tablet resting upon the air.

This is all we know of the Ionic School. Their investigations related to matter rather than to mind; they extl.

plained all things principally by matter. They were generally called Physicists.

Their method, though empirical, differed from the Baconian. They rose from few facts to the general law; Bacon employed many facts, and rose slowly to the general law. The theories of this school harmonize in this, that the aëriform liquid and the solid substances are mutually related, and one springs from the other, and that they sought the origin of things in the elements.

Next arose

B.—The Pythagorean School.

This school was Dorian. It attempted a higher solution of the problem—"What is the original of all things?" The proportions and dimensions of matter, rather than its sensible concretions, seemed to them to furnish the true explanation of being. They accordingly adopted as the principle of their philosophy that which would express a quantitative determination of proportions, namely, numbers, but disregarded qualitative determinateness. "Number is the essence of all things," was their position.

1. Pythagoras (540-500 B.C.) To him is referred this doctrine of numbers. He was born at Samos, at an uncertain date. Numerous fables say that he drew his descent from the Pelasgians. He traveled in Egypt, and was initiated into the mysteries of the Egyptian priests. During the latter part of his life he lived at Crotona, in Magna Grecia. Many curious legends are related about him. It is said that a halo encircled his head, and that he had a golden thigh. Wild beasts obeyed his call. He claimed to be omniscient and ubiquitous, and to hold converse with a river god; in particular, he affirmed that Hermes gave him the power of recollecting his past existence, and of imparting this power to others. At Crotona he founded a society or order for the moral and political regeneration of the lower Italian cities, planning to rule them by means of the highest intellects. Through this society this new philosophy seems to have been introduced, though more as a mode ot life than in the form of a scientific theory. He thought that the first step towards wisdom was the study of mathematics, a sci-

ence which contemplates objects, that is, numbers, which are both corporeal and incorporeal beings, and, as it were, on the border land between the two; a science which most advantageously inures the mind to contemplation. He himself was at the head of a mathematical and political school which he had instituted. He held a very severe examination of students applying for entrance; he made a special examination of their physiognomies; then, after entrance, he enjoined silence for some years (a secret society).

The most probable explanation of the Pythagorean doctrine of numbers is that they are used as symbolical or emblematical representations of the first principles and forms of nature, and particularly of those immutable and eternal essences to which Plato afterwards gave the appellation of Ideas. Not being able, or not choosing, to explain in simple language the abstract notions of principles and forms, Pythagoras seems to have made use of numbers as geometricians make use of diagrams, to assist the conceptions of scholars. More particularly, on account of the analogy between numbers and intelligent forms, which subsist in the Divine mind, he made the former a symbol of the latter. He thought that the universe, as a simple system, was generated out of numbers, that is, revolved from west to east; the bodies moving in a regular dance. Of this universe, fire holds the middle place; or in the midst of the four elements is placed the fiery globe of unity. The earth is not without motion; nor is it situated in the centre of the spheres, but is one of those planets which make their revolutions about the sphere of fire.

Copernicus admits that this suggested to him the solar system with the sun in the centre. Gravitation made a law of numbers.

One of the curious doctrines of Pythagoras was that of the transmigration of souls, metempsychosis, which was the cause of the abstinence of the Pythagoreans from animal food, and of the exclusion of animal sacrifices from their religious ceremonies. This doctrine necessitated a belief in the immortality of the soul.

People could not believe that the soul died with the body, and as it must be somewhere, they believed that it passed from one body to another. All knowledge is recol-

lection, and, by extension of the argument, we must have been in a future state.

Among his followers were Archytus (504–460 B. C.) and Philolaus.

The whole tendency of the Pythagorean philosophy was in a practical respect ascetic, and directed to a strict culture of the character.

Views of the Pythagorean School.

"ἀρχή—number—the essence of things—everything is number," (Aristotle.) To be taken in the (1) material sense, viz., numbers are the origin of things, and (McCosh) things are the copies of numbers; (2) formal sense, viz., numbers are the archetypes of things. Grote says that numbers were not separate from things, but fundamental in things.

Properties of numbers:

One, or μόνος=determining and indeterminate.

Odd numbers=determining.

Even numbers=indeterminate.

The first 4 numbers=10.

The first 4 odd numbers=16.

A mystic importance was attached to the number seven. The fundamental conceptions of geometry correspond to the first four numbers, *e. g.*, 1=point, 2=line, 3=surface, 4=geometrical body; further 5=color, visible appearance, etc. Geometrical forms were identified with physical objects; *e. g.*, a cube=earth, dodecahedron=water, and pyramid=fire.

Pythagoras discovered the mathematical relations of music. He was led to it by hearing the ring of the blacksmith's hammer.

The universe was a single system generated out of numbers; the world, a closed ball with a central point of fire, called the hearth of the universe, or watch-tower of Zeus. Around this centre were three divine globes; (1) κόσμος, reaching from earth to heaven. (2) The space from the moon to the fixed stars. (3) The space from the fixed stars to Olympus, the seat of the gods. Within the outer sphere of fixed stars, composed of fire, like the centre, were ten bodies performing a regular dance, from which came the music of the spheres. In (" 2") were Saturn, Jupiter, Mars, Venus, Mercury. In ("1") were the Sun, Moon, and Earth. Between the earth and the central fire was a counter earth, imagined to make up the round number ten. This was called Antichthon.

There were ten categories or contraries to which the actual varieties of the sensible world might be reduced—

1. Limited and Unlimited.
2. Odd and Even.
3. One and Many.
4. Right and Left.
5. Male and Female.
6. Rest and Motion.
7. Straight and Curved.
8. Light and Darkness.
9. Good and Evil.
10. Square and Oblong.

C.—The Eleatic School.

The philosophers of this school step absolutely beyond what is given by experience, and make a complete abstraction of everything material. This abstraction, the negation of all division in space and time, they take as their principle, and call it pure being. The Ionians, as a school, held this to be a mere sensuous principle; the Pythagoreans, that it was a symbolic principle; but the Eleatics reject these views, and make as the fundamental thought the negation of everything posterior and exterior. Only being is, and there is no not-being nor becoming. This being is the purely undetermined, changeless ground of all things. It is not being in becoming, but it is being as exclusive of all becoming; in other words, it is pure being. This view of being led to monism.

The question arises here, was Greek Philosophy original, or was it derived from an eastern source? Dr. McCosh thinks it original. Others say that the earliest philosophy was found nearer the east, and so there must have been a philosophy in India, Syria, and Egypt. Also as the Greeks got their letters from Phenicia, so they got their

philosophy there also. There is no evidence that they got it from India. There was a philosophy in India, but it was very vague. It is doubtful whether Babylon or Syria had a philosophic system, or even whether Egypt had, although there was a religion constructed by the priests, who held to metempsychosis, which was adopted by Protagoras and Plato. This, however, was a belief common to the entire east. Yet just as Homer may have had precursors who influenced him, so Greek philosophy may have felt the influence of other lands, yet if so the Greeks assimilated and made thoroughly their own whatever thought they took.

Another important question arises,—how do we learn of the Pre-Socratic schools?

People spoke in parables and wrote in poetry. Fragments of Xenophanes, of Xeno, and several hundred lines of Empedocles is extant.

Most important sources of knowledge, however, are:—

1. Aristotle, who often prefaced his treatises with an account of his predecessors, written in a fault-finding vein. He, however, understood their philosophy.
2. Diogenes Laertius wrote a History of Philosophy, but did not understand philosophy, and so is reliable only when he quotes.
3. Cicero, who gave an exact account of many philosophers, with quotations and Greek terms. He understood their philosophy and strove to deal with them honestly.
4. There exist commentaries on Aristotle.
5. Plutarch, the historian, or, as some think, the pseudo Plutarch.
6. Proclus.
7. The Christian Fathers quote largely. Thus from 600–500 we know that three schools of great thinkers appeared, the Physicists, the Mathematicians and the Eleatics.

This school is called the Eleatic because it arose in Elea, in Lucania, a country of Magna Græcia. It was founded 450 B. C. The philosophers of this school were—

1. Xenophanes (born 536 B. C.) is considered as the originator of the Eleatic tendency. He was born at Colophon, and emigrated to Elea, a Phœnician country in Lucania.

He was a younger contemporary of Pythagoras. Indulging, however, in a greater freedom of thought than was usual among the disciples of Pythagoras, he ventured to introduce new opinions of his own, and in many particulars to oppose the doctrine of Epimenides, Thales, and Pythagoras. Like Homer, he was a rhapsodist, and his writings are characterized by something similar to Homer's power. He wrote a poem, some one hundred lines of which are preserved. As we read them we are filled with a sort of astonishment at his power. He considered matter as a thing of opinion, and set but little value on the inquiry whether there was such a thing as matter or not. His inquiry was περὶ φύσεως. He appears to have first uttered the proposition, "Everything is one"—ἓν καὶ πᾶν; without, however, giving any more explicit determination respecting this unity, whether it is one simply in conception or in actuality. All his arguments are divided into two heads :

(1.) God is all powerful and unchangeable, and the very essence of things. "This Deity," he said, "could not have originated out of like or unlike: for if from the former, it would be the same, and if from the latter, it would be the weaker; hence it could not have originated at all. This was taking high and exalted views of God. He said that if lions or oxen could paint, they would represent their gods as lions or oxen. The Ethiopians conceive of their gods as black; the Thracians, as fair and with reddish hair. He, in particular, denounced the teaching of Homer and Hesiod, who sang of the robbery, adultery, and deceit of the gods, charging these poets with having led the people to worship low things. In his poem he looks at the Godhead as wholly seeing, understanding, hearing, unmoved, undivided, calmly ruling all things by his thought; as one incorporeal, eternal being, spherical in form like the universe. He says that God is of the same nature as the universe, comprehending all things within himself, pervading all things, but bearing no resemblance to man either in body or mind. He did not distinguish between the creature and the creator.

(2.) The denial of all beginning of being. He taught that if there ever had been a time when nothing existed, nothing could ever have existed; that whatever is, always

has been from eternity, without deriving its existence from any prior principle; that nature is one and without limit: that what is one is similar in all its parts, else it would be many; that the one infinite, eternal, and homogeneous universe is immutable and incapable of change. He can, perhaps, hardly be called a pantheist, but still he did not perceive the difference between God, the Being and the created.

He did not distinguish between *πράττω* and *ποιέω*. He would reckon the works of God, not merely as his works, but as the very essence of God. The works of nature, he said, are as parts of God He says, "Everything is one." Contemplating the world as a whole he names the unity which he finds, God. He denied the Pythagorean doctrine of metempsychosis. No doubt Xenophanes directed his scholars to the highest wisdom, but along with the essential being he held some strange opinions. He maintained the unity of thought and being, saying that to be and to think are the same. His fundamental tenet was partly religious and partly philosophical, a sort of pantheism or pancosmism. *Non ens* is with him an absurdity. He had two methods by which he constantly expressed himself, his *λόγος* and *δόξα*. The former meant highest reason; the latter, matters of opinion. Some things he said we could not regard as essential truth.

He distinguished between *νοῦς* and *αἴσθησις*. The former alone gives us truth, the latter deceive us and so we must go back to *νοῦς* and *λόγος*. This school had a sort of physical science discovered by *δόξα*. It discovered water and earth, and by these explained the universe. Yet there was no certainty in it. We do not know the realities of things.

2. Parmenides, (519–460 B. C.) He is at the proper head of the Eleatic School a scholar, or, at least, an adherent of Xenophanes. He was born at Elea. At the age of sixty-five he came to Athens, where he met Socrates, with whom he conversed on the doctrine of ideas (according to Plato.)

He embodied his philosophy in an epic poem on "Nature," of which we still have important fragments. It opens with an allegory which was intended to exhibit the soul's longing after truth. The soul is represented as drawn along an untrodden road to the residence of Justice (Δίκη), who promises to reveal everything to him. After the introduction, the work is divided into two parts; the first treats of the knowledge of truth, and the second explains the physiological system of the Eleatic School. He holds two theories—

(1.) A Theory of Truth.

(2.) A Theory of Opinion.

He drew a distinction between decisions, perception, and intelligence (αἴσθησις and λόγος). Thus we have a distinction between the material and the non-material. (1.) All being is full of thought. (2.) The notion that being is imperishable.

The grand principle of his whole philosophy is, that non-being is inconceivable; he held, therefore, that there could be no vacuum; and he was led, therefore, to the denial of all motion and change—all was thought and intelligence, without change or limit. He maintained that all space was occupied with being. As duration and extension are really indivisible, though divided into hours and miles for convenience; so being, though divisible in matter, changeable, etc., is really continuous and immutable. The existing has never come into being, nor is it perishable; there is neither past nor future, but all came from the same, and is included in the present. As every coming into existence presupposes a non-existence, therefore there could be no coming into existence. He identifies ὁ νοῦς and τὸ ὄν, thought and being. The Hegelians say that his τὸ ὄν, etc., was an anticipation of their doctrine.

There is a difference between Xenophanes and Parmenides. With the former, the essential being, τὸ ὄν, was God; with the latter, the principle was a metaphysical power or form. Along with his view of being, Parmenides had also a view of nature—but this became merely a matter of probability. In the second part of his poem he makes an attempt to explain the phenomenal world, and give it a physical derivation. Though firmly convinced that according to reason and conception, there is only "the one," yet he is unable to withdraw himself from the recognition of an appearing manifoldness and change. He explained the phenomena of nature from the mingling of two

unchangeable elements, which Aristotle, though apparently only by way of example, indicates as warm and cold, fire and earth. Concerning these two elements, Aristotle remarks still further, that Parmenides united the warmth with being, and the other element with non-being.

3. Zeno (490 B. C.), a philosopher of Elea, called the Eleatic, to distinguish him from Zeno, the Stoic. He was the disciple of Parmenides, and was the earliest (?) prose writer among the Grecian philosophers. He is represented by Aristotle as the first to introduce dialectic discussions—something like our modern speculative philosophy. His ingenuity seems to have been shown in arguing against those who opposed the Eleatic School. He was a firm defender of the fathers of the school. The main object of his writings was to prove that there is a contradiction in the very idea of motion. He endeavored to show this by the famous example of Achilles and the tortoise. He says there can be no such thing as motion for these reasons:

(1.) On account of the infinite divisibility of space and matter; for in order to the beginning of motion a body must pass over an infinite space in finite time.

(2.) Because the slow cannot be overtaken by the swift.

(3.) The same body must be in motion and, at the same time, at rest.

(4.) One and the same space might be both long and short.

But we may easily reconcile all these by taking time and motion together.

According to Aristotle, Zeno taught that nothing can be produced either from that which is similar or dissimilar; that there is only one being, and that is God; that this being is eternal, homogeneous, and spherical, neither finite nor infinite; neither quiescent nor movable; that there are many worlds; that there is in nature no vacuum.

His intention was probably to defend the doctrines of his teachers, and show that these could not be denied without running into difficulties and contradictions.

If Seneca's account of this philosopher deserves credit, he reached the highest point of scepticism, and denied the existence of external objects.

Some of Zeno's arguments were antinomies, deducing from the same premises an affirmative and a negative conclusion.

4. Melissus, of Samos, maintained that there was neither vacuum nor any such thing as production or decay, and that the changes going on are but illusions of the senses. Then do not trust to the senses: trust to the λόγος.

D.—The Intermediate School.

This is between the early school and Socrates. There is no impropriety in this language. They may be called intermediate because they cannot be put in either of those mentioned before. Here it will be well to consider the relation of this school to the Eleatics. Being and existence, the one and the many, could not be united by the principle of the Eleatics. The Monism which they had striven for had resulted in an ill-concealed Dualism. Heraclitus reconciled this contradiction by affirming that being and not-being, the one and the many, existed at the same time as the *becoming*. While the Eleatics could not extricate themselves from the dilemma that the world is either being or not-being, this intermediate school removes the difficulty by answering: "It is neither being nor not-being, because it is both."

2. Anaxagoras—born at Clazomenæ, 500 B. C., a date which is inconsistent, however, with his reputed friendship with Pericles. He is said to have gone to Athens soon after the Persian war, and to have lived and taught there a long time; thus transferring philosophy to that place. His connection, however, with the powerful of the Athenians, profited but little; for not only does he seem to have passed his old age in poverty, but he was not even safe from the persecution which assailed the friends of Pericles on the decline of his power. He was accused of impiety towards the gods, thrown into prison, and eventually forced to flee to Lampsacus, where he died at the age of seventy-two. Some foundation for the charge of impiety was probably found in his general views, which, undoubtedly, were far from according with the popular notions of

religion, since he regarded the sun and moon as consisting of earth and stone; and miraculous indications at sacrifices as ordinary appearances of nature.

From his time onward, Athens became the centre of intellectual life in Greece. From his intimate acquaintance with Pericles, and other Athenians of high rank, he exerted a decisive influence upon the culture of his age. He had a work on nature written in poetry. He occupied himself much with mathematics and the kindred sciences; especially Astronomy, as the character of the discoveries attributed to him sufficiently shows. He is represented as having conjectured the right explanation of the moon's light and of the solar and lunar eclipses. It is said, also, that he could see in the moon plains, mountains, and even human habitations.

He accounted for chance as that of which we do not know the cause. He sets up the idea of a world-forming intelligence, *νοῦς*, absolutely separated from all matter and working with design. He speculated on things as infinite in number and different in species; but above these he places a moving principle, *νοῦς*, intellect, and to this he assigns the organization of all things. We are not certain what he meant. His views are much criticised by the ancients, especially by Socrates and Aristotle, because his doctrine is of such a mechanical nature or character. Socrates condemns him for calling in other elements besides the *νοῦς*. He admits mind as the ultimate ground of all things, yet only resorts to it for the explanation of phenomena whose necessity he could not derive from the casuality in nature. Anaxagoras, therefore, rather postulated than proved mind as an energy above nature and as the truth and actuality of natural being. Still, I think he had a slight glimpse of what has since been revealed in modern science, viz., that God works through nature. The whole nature of the man leads us to think that by *νοῦς* he meant God. Whether he gave the *νοῦς* a separate place, or called it in with others, has yet to be settled. No Greek philosopher fully settled what came to be known afterwards. Greek philosophy never had any idea of creation.

Ideas due to Anaxagoras:

(1) Idea of seeds, τὰ ὁμοιομερῆ. They were infinite in number; of different species, which were not interchangeable, though each contained in a latent state the germs of all the rest. An aggregation of a number of these seeds of some one kind formed a body of definite proportions and chemical equivalents.

(2) Doctrine of chance rejected. He affirmed τύχη to be undiscoverable by human reason.

(3) Mysteriousness of nature, arising from the uncertainty of knowledge and untrustworthiness of the senses.

(4) The organizing νοῦς.

1. Heraclitus, a native of Ephesus, surnamed the Naturalist (ὁ φυσικός) and belongs to the dynamical school of Ionian philosophy. He flourished about 500 B. C., and died in the sixtieth year of his age. He assumed the title of "self-taught" (αὐτο διδακτός); for being an aristocrat by birth, he was too proud to acknowledge the services of any. He was the founder of the "Flux" school.

He wrote a work on nature which was laden with apothegms, and very much in the style of Bacon, but so obscure that it gained for him the name of "the obscure." He says the end of wisdom is to discover the ground and principle of all things, which he said was fire;—not flame, but hot air, or vapor, of which flame was simply the excess. This "principle" is a universal agent with no limits to its activity; therefore nothing that it forms is fixed, and consequently all things are constantly destroyed and reformed. All is in a state of flux. We are all disposed of by Fate (=God). The world is to be destroyed by heat, and out of this is to come a new world. This doctrine tinged his philosophy with melancholy. He said that birth is a calamity because death is in life, and life is in death. He identified fire with God, and made necessity rule. Fire is self-enkindled and self-extinguished. On the ground of flux he denied the credibility of the senses which reveal a continuance, while in reality all is change.

2. Empedocles, (500–440 B. C.) a native of Agrigentum, in Sicily, was a priest and a prophet. He is said to have

2 Thame ...

1, ...

The ... was ...

all the ...

committed suicide by throwing himself into Etna. He wrote a doctrinal poem concerning nature, of which only 444 lines remain. His philosophy seems to be a mixture of the Ionic and Pythagorean schools. He describes man as an erring fugitive and vagabond on earth, having fallen from high dignity.

He taught that originally all was one; that God was eternal and at rest. He was the first philosopher to recognize the four elements, earth, air, water and fire; and from this time down these four elements play an active and prominent part in all speculations. We find them all combined. All things are under one of these forms; either fiery, watery, solid, or gaseous. He combines air and water; fire as the rarest and most powerful, he held to be the chief, and consequently the soul of all sentient and intelligent beings, which issue from the central fire or soul of the world. He gives the fullest account of the physiological side. Operating upon these four elements he thought of two active powers, love and hate, called in modern philosophical language, attraction and repulsion.

We have, then, the activities of nature now introduced, love (φιλία) "undying friendship," and hate, (νεῖκος) or "dividing strife." The elements of things are held together in undistinguishable confusion by love, the primal force which unites like to like. In a portion of this whole, however, or, as he expresses it, in the members of the Deity, which he held to be a sphere and a mixture—σφαῖρος μῖγμα—without a vacuum, strife, νεῖκος, the force which binds like to unlike prevailed, and gave the elements a tendency to separate themselves, whereby the first became perceptible as such: although the separation was not so complete, but that each contained portions of the others. Hence arose the multiplicity of things. By the vivifying counteraction of love, organic life was produced; not, however, so perfect and so full of design as it now appears; but, at first, single limbs, then irregular combinations, till ultimately they received their present adjustments and perfection. But as the forces of love and hate are constantly acting on each other for generation and destruction, the present condition of things cannot properly persist, or combine forever, and the world which properly is not the all, but only the ordered part of it, will again be reduced to a chaotic unity, out of which a new system will be formed, and so on forever. There is no real distinction of anything, but only a change of combinations. From all bodies minute particles are thrown off by repulsion.

No philosopher of his time recognized an intelligent Creator. Some say the Shemitic race had a faint idea of it; but this is very doubtful. Revelation alone gives it.

He laid down the doctrine, "*similia similibus percipiuntur*," like is perceived by like. He held that the substances themselves differ. In the impure separation of the elements, it is only the predominant one that the senses can apprehend, and consequently, though man can know all the elements of the whole singly, he is unable to see them in their perfect unity, wherein consists their truth. Empedocles, therefore, rejects the testimony of the senses, and maintains that pure intellect can arrive at a knowledge of the truth. His moral doctrine is of a high character. He had a knowledge of sin, and made a distinction between good and evil. "Man is a fallen demon." "I am an erring, wandering one." As to the soul of man he called it a form, a quintessence of the four elements. He held that the soul migrated through animal and vegetable bodies, in atonement for some guilt committed in its unembodied state, when it is a demon, of which he supposes an infinite number existed. Hence he maintained the doctrine of the transmigration of souls, or as he called them, "forms." He said that he himself had been in all forms. Mind was from all eternity.

He forbade his followers to eat animal food; was he the founder of Buddhism? There is an anticipation by the Eleatics of the doctrine of the conservation of energy.

E.—The Atomic School.

1. Leucippus is generally believed to be the founder of the school. He was born about 500 B. C. He held the existence of a vacuum; in it were atoms, infinite in number, and diverse in forms. According to him "the soul was a mass of wind atoms." He distinguished between primary

and secondary qualities of matter. He tended towards atheism.

Democritus, the founder and most illustrious of the school, was the son of rich parents, and was born about 460 B. C., in Abdera, an Ionian colony. He is represented as the most learned and varied in attainments before the time of Aristotle. He has been much studied in our time through the influence of Grote. He belongs to the school of Comte.

His teachings were as follows:

1. From nothing, nothing comes. Nothing that exists can be destroyed. All changes are due to the combination and separation of atoms.
2. Nothing happens by chance: every occurrence has its *αἰτία*.
3. We have only atoms and the empty space in which they move. All else is mere opinion.
4. Atoms are infinite in number and variation of form. They have lateral motions and whirling motions, and when they strike that is the origin of the world.
5. The varieties of all things depend on the varieties of their constituent atoms.
6. The soul consists of three smooth round atoms, very mobile, interpenetrating the whole body; and from the combination of these comes sensation.

With him, time, space, and motion, were all eternal. The atoms are ever whirling, and their movements produce order, while some, more immaterial than others, produced mind. He resolved all knowledge, all sensuous cogitations into contact. Death consisted not in the destruction of these atoms. He also believed that if there were a God, he consisted of these fiery atoms. He introduced the hypothesis of images, (*εἴδωλα*), a species of emanation from external objects, which make an impression on our senses, and from the influence of which he deduced sensation and thought. These emanations were thrown off and then seized by the mind, or, as he called it, aggregate of these atoms. Sight and hearing accordingly arise from the impression of a foreign body on the soul. He is therefore the founder of the ideal theory of sense-perception. He held thus that all bodies were sending off images, (Grote calls them "effluvia,") emanations of some kind; these were material, and reached the soul and were detained and then perceived. This is the doctrine of *mediate perception.*

This lead to a more ethereal theory, that sensation was a mere idea in the mind (Descartes and Locke). This was opposed by Reid and Hamilton.

This doctrine (of atoms) of Democritus has been held by many from his time to ours. The Epicureans held it. Lucretius, an atheist, adopted it, and expounded it with great ability. The Stoics also professed it.

Democritus did not deny the presence of a God, although his system does. Bacon showed that the atomic theory is not necessarily atheistic, for the forms into which the atoms are thrown argue something behind with a plan, and also that these atoms were created. So Chalmers and Mill say there must have been an arranging power. Newton adopted the molecular theory in another form. The dynamical theory is connected with it. Atoms, if they exist, must be very small.

REMARKS ON THE PRE-SOCRATIC SCHOOL.

1. *Method.* This is essential in all philosophical treatises. It is called by Bacon empirical, mingled with analytical and *a priori* method. The Rationalists draw entirely on their reason, while the Empiricists make use of facts. They desired, but they failed, to construct a system on a few facts. They (the Pre-Socratic philosophers) made a few observations but no experiments. They separated things in thought, and they constructed them *a priori.*

2. *As to God* they were more or less pantheists. None of them were atheists. None of them believed in a creation. All believed in something coeval and co-equal with God. Some identified God with water, others with fire, etc. Democritus made him of fire. Many held that he was a metaphysical being.

3. They separated God from His works.

4. Their speculations on moral subjects were dim and obscure.

5. Their view and speculation of the *immortality of the soul.* They entertained the doctrine of metempsychosis—

Ocean & T[illegible]

thro[illegible]

[illegible]

of those who believed that the soul was fire. Some thought it was lost as such at death, others that it was absorbed into the Divine Being. Their object was to discover truth. The Greeks came to the conclusion that the senses deceive us; to discover the truth was to go deeper than the surface. Their aim generally was to find the cause of things. One said the world was derived from a certain principle, the name of which was unknown. Some called it ἀρχή; some found it in water, others in air, still others in fire.

The Sophists.

Thought now comes into collision and sects begin to contend, thus creating an interest. Now there arose a different class of speculators in Asia, Elea, the south of Italy and other places. At the period of about 450 B. C. we find a great activity of thought at Elea, Miletus, Ephesus, and other places. Out of these cities arose a set of men called the Sophists.

These were—

Protagoras of Abdera, 440 B. C., Relativity.
Gorgias of Leontina, Nihilist.
Polus of Agrigentum, Polytheist.
Hippias of Elis, Polytheist.
Prodicus of Cos, Moralist.
Thrasymachus of Chalcedon.
Euthydemus of Chios, } Brothers.
Dionysodorus " " }
Antiphon of Athens.

These Sophists became professors, teachers, tutors, or, in modern language, lecturers, going from town to town and giving instruction. They professed to be teachers of the young. At length they settled in Athens. They did not prescribe any fee, but said "Give the value of what knowledge you receive." They had no desire to inculcate the truth, but simply taught a man to be able to know something of other men's opinions. They taught that a man may defend either a bad or a good cause. Their style has ever been called "sophistic."

We have accounts given of them in the "Memorabilia," in Aristotle, and in the dialogues of Plato. Since that time it has been customary to speak of them in disparaging terms. A "sophist" is a term of reproach. By a sophistical mind is meant one that does not want to know the truth, and does everything conceivable and artful to keep others from knowing it.

In later times, however, attempts have been made to defend these Sophists. Lewes says that we have accounts of them only from their enemies, and must not receive them. Grote also defends the Sophists. He says the word Sophist might have applied to Socrates himself.

This has given rise to a keen discussion in our times, and we will now enter to some degree into it. The charges against the Sophists are:

1. That they taught for money. The defence is that all professors in modern times teach for money. The mere idea of reward had never entered the head of the Sophist. It is said in their behalf that, while they did expect pay, they made no legal demand for it. Yet it is to be said that, although they did not make a special charge, still a remuneration was expected, in proportion to the good they had done. Their remuneration, then, was not a fixed sum. And the Sophists, therefore, were in this respect free from charge.

2. That they taught scepticism in religion and in all things. This charge has some foundation of truth; not that they were really sceptics, but that they had no belief in anything. The men of the world began to look into many philosophies, and pronounced them ingenious speculations: so far then, they did not profess to know the truth. There arose men who said that it was impossible to distinguish between truth and error.

3. That they taught many wrong principles of morals. There were, however, some good points. Grote denies the charge, and shows from the fable of "The choice of Hercules," which we owe to Prodicus, that they did teach correct principles in morals. It is difficult to reach the truth of this matter. But that they taught a corrupt morality is not to be believed; if so, parents would not have sent to them their children: but still no true, high principle of morality. The tendency of the system was to efface all distinction between truth and error. A young man might practice either of these. They taught, however, liberality.

They [illegible] to [illegible]
of Garden.
Pfale [illegible] install
[illegible] them.

[illegible] as [illegible]
[illegible]
[illegible] little [illegible]

2 They did not mean
[illegible] that

4. That they did not seek to inculcate the truth in the minds of their scholars, (but taught them to defend either side of a question ;) in short, that they were merely professional men. Hippias is said to have defended one side of a question, and then to turn around and argue the other.

5. That their sole business was to promote immorality among the young. This charge can be made. It was not necessary for them to be bad men, yet theirs were not lives of wisdom. They did not teach the young to be good, to seek after truth; but to seek what could make them the most brilliant; for then they would get along well in the world. The tendency of the system thus is to deface the distinction between good and evil as well as between truth and error.

6. That they were men to defend or learn to defend what which they did not believe. These are sophists, and their doctrine is "sophistic." Their inquiry generally was: "What is the most ingenious opinion ?"

The apostle says the Greeks were seeking after wisdom: not that he condemned wisdom; but the *σοφία* of Paul evidently means this wisdom of the Greeks in comparison with the true. The wisdom which he seeks is a peculiar one; their wisdom was not truth.

What truth is there in these objections? In regard to the first, Christ lays down the rule that "the laborer is worthy of his hire." The second can hardly be proven. The third is most likely untrue. As to the fourth, in that respect they differ from all the older and contemporary philosophers. Their object was not to look after the truth but only to advance their cause, and so they fall back on Agnosticism.

Protagoras was the most illustrious of these, and his doctrine was "Man is the measure of all things, both of that which exists and of that which does not." In regard to this, Plato says: "They derive all knowledge from *αἴσθησις*, and resolve all things into sensation; and his own sensation is to each individual his measure of truth." Again, Protagoras says: "I can know nothing concerning the gods, whether they exist or not, for we are prevented from gaining such knowledge, not only by the obscurity of the thing itself, but by the shortness of the human life.

Grote has developed a theory of relativity which he ascribes to Protagoras: "Object is implicated with, limited by, and measured by subject. The mind mixes itself up with the object. As things appear to you, so they are to you; as they appear to me, so they are to me." Grote says as far as the doctrine asserts implication of mind with object, it is true.

He proposes another: "What is true to one man is often false to another. That which is treated as infallible truth in one part of the globe has nothing to do with the other part; and when man speaks the truth he only says what an individual thinks is true." Thus says Grote, in relation to this second charge.

We are surprised to find Grote repeating such jargon concerning "subject and object." We cannot argue from the existence of mind that there must be something to think about; just as we cannot argue that every woman has a husband because there are such things as husbands. We cannot say what is the precise principle or doctrine of the Sophists, or whether they had any or not. The fatal part of the Sophistic doctrine is that truth varies with the individual. Human knowledge is often partial, but truth is the agreement of thoughts with things. If any one were to affirm that there is no such country as Greece, or that Hayes is not President of the United States, or that Washington never lived, he would be in error. "Still," says Grote, "no infallible evidence has yet been found." We cannot obtain what a certain school calls "absolute truth." It is said to seek for certain criteria. They did not teach truth. We have a test, however, to find what is truth and what is error, but we will not exhibit it here.

Gorgias the nihilist, held under that name what is now called Agnosticism. His statement is: Nothing exists. If it does exist, it is unknowable. If it exists and is cognizable, yet it cannot be communicated to others.

Hippias was distinguished principally for his rhetorical talent, and is the exponent of Sophistical Ethics. Prodicus was also a teacher of Rhetoric, and was principally noted for his "Choice of Hercules." He was also fond of discriminating between synonyms. He also treated somewhat of Ethics. Of the other Sophists we know almost nothing.

CHAPTER II.

II.—COMBINED SCHOOLS UNDER SOCRATES, PLATO, ARISTOTLE.

A.—Socrates.

The period we have just passed over is that of the "Scattered Schools." Now come the "Combined Schools." Socrates was the result of a reaction. He was a man of great acuteness and humor, which he delighted to exercise. He was opposed to pretense of any kind, and began to doubt whether the sophists really possessed wisdom.

He was born at Alopece, a village near Athens, in the year 469 B. C. He died 399 B. C. His parents were of low rank. His father was a statuary, his mother a midwife; the former was named Sophroniscus, the latter Phænarete. In order to understand his philosophy we must know his personal character and history. To his personal character especially does he owe much of his greatness. His personal appearance was by no means prepossessing. He is described as being short, with a flat nose and corpulent body. From the first he was a remarkable man, and gave himself to deep thoughts. He was a man of great affection and attractions for the young. His great desire was to pull down and destroy the false theories of others. He never accepted compliments, was unselfish, and was never swayed by the love of money. Wherever he appeared he was surrounded by a crowd of listeners. He used to say, "I follow the profession of my mother, and my business is to draw truth from you and not to put it into you; it is in you if you only knew it." He put many questions, and would have many different answers from his pupils; thus he would test them by making them contradict themselves.

He loved to meet with a Sophist, as with Gorgias, and lead him onward under pretence of learning something. Socrates would ask Gorgias: "What is eloquence, beauty?" and then harder questions, in order to get him to contradict himself, and thus throw him into confusion. When he came to a school he would assume the attitude of ignorance, and apparently would let himself be instructed by those with whom he conversed; then he would put a series of questions, such as: "You said so and so?" "Yes." "And have you not said so and so?" "Yes." "But these two do not agree." So he would land them in perpetual difficulties and confusion. This was his "irony" (*εἰρωνεία*).

Now as to the circumstances under which he was educated. He seems to have been first a physicist, that is, of the Ionic school. His admiration of Pythagoras was great. But at length he became dissatisfied with their materialism and turned his attention from physics and endeavored to call away men's attention from these to better and higher inquiries. He turned his attention to moral subjects, and as Cicero says, "brought down philosophy from heaven to earth."

In his method there are some peculiarities. There is a sort of scepticism—not to say or understand, however, that he meant to undermine all truth, but that he said it was difficult to distinguish between truth and error. He was distinguished for his love of truth, and even believed in a God. He said that what was said to be truth was not all truth. He differed from the sophists in this, that they said truth cannot be found, so let us turn our attention to what will be of use hereafter. Socrates said truth is difficult to find, but it is the business of life to find it.

Our knowledge of Socrates is derived from two sources or views, Xenophon and Plato. In Xenophon's "Memorabilia" we have him represented as a man of great ability and common sense; a man of integrity, just and affable. And yet we have not the whole of the man, because Xenophon could not rightly appreciate him as a philosopher. In Plato we have described his delicate subtlety and skill in questioning; hence we find him dealing with the highest problems. Still we are not sure how much is to be ascribed to the master and how much to the pupil.

He was brought up [illegible]
[illegible]
the [illegible] moral [illegible]
[illegible]
[illegible]

[illegible]
[illegible]
With a [illegible]
[illegible]
[illegible]
[illegible]

[illegible]

Now some may say these two views are different. But he was distinguished for virtue and also for wisdom in search after truth. Each man or historian gave what he understood; one did not appreciate dialectic subjects, and hence we can trust Xenophon as a historian. But Plato was a lover of the dialectics; hence he appreciated something that Xenophon could not. We cannot, therefore, get the true Socrates by reading one and not the other. Just as in the life of Christ, the first three Gospels do not give a complete view; a fourth must be added as a supplement. But John writes as he was inspired; not so Plato. Of the latter's views concerning Socrates we must not be too certain.

Before entering upon the study of the Philosophy of Socrates, let us take a brief review, and fix in our minds exactly where we are.

We have seen that there were different schools in these early ages, and many philosophers.

1. There were those who sought the ἀρχή in some physical power, as air, water, etc.

2. There were those who thought they could reduce it to the "Harmonics of Nature."

3. There arose the metaphysical school—passing from things that change to things that never change.

4. There arose an intermediate school and also an Atomic school.

5. There arose a professional school, introduced by the Sophists.

6. At this state of affairs arose Socrates.

THE PHILOSOPHY OF SOCRATES AND PLATO.

I.—Socrates.

A.—*Method.* This was avowedly dialectic, which he got from Zeno, the Eleatic. He thought everything should be looked at and discussed in various lights. Dialectics corresponded somewhat with modern speculative philosophy. It is difficult to define it. He was not satisfied with things as they appeared, but wanted to know them as they are, to know the τὸ ὄν, τὸ εἶναι. This is not, as the Germans say, the *Absolute*, but the *Real.*

Dialectics has a two-fold character—negative and positive. The negative is the well-known Socratic "irony," εἰρωνεία. The result of this was only to lead the subject to know that he knew nothing; and the great many of the dialogues of Xenophon go no further than to represent this negative result. The positive side is the so-called obstetrics, or art of intellectual midwifery. Socrates compares himself with his mother, Phaenarete, a midwife, because his position was rather to help others bring forth thoughts than to produce them himself. Through this art of midwifery he, by his assiduous questioning, by his interrogating dissection of the notions of him with whom he might be conversing, elicited thought which had hitherto been inactive.

Aristotle says Socrates introduced definition and division, genus and species. These two, definition and division, were the foundation of his philosophy. He enquired into the nature of things, proceeding by definition and division. Some have said that he proceeded by Induction. This must not be understood to be the same as Bacon's method, nor that he anticipated Bacon at all. Socrates, starting from some of the most concrete cases, and seizing hold of some of the most concrete notions, and finding illustrations in the most trivial occurrences, knew how to remove, by his comparisons, that which was individual: by thus separating the accidental and contingent from the essential, he could bring up to consciousness a universal truth and determination: in other words, could form conceptions. Hence, he appealed to facts only as examples. For instance, to inquire into beauty, justice or valor, he would start from individual examples of them, and from these deduce the universal character or conception of these virtues.

Thus his method was not a gathering of facts, as he took only the individual thing. He called it the obstetric method.

But, further, he enquired also what things are in themselves, discussing them according to their genus and species.

B.—*Doctrine.* Now by this method he inquired into two things:

1. The *providence* of God (*πρόνοια*). He had very high views on this subject; he not only believed in a God, but that everything in the world was ordered and taken care of by him. He appealed to the supernatural, and supposed it guided him in all things, believing that it gave him intimations even in spiritual affairs. He hardly knew what this *δαιμόνιον*, as he called it, was; but, by looking within, and by cultivating humility and toleration, the *δαιμόνιον* could be invoked and known. He seems to imply, however, that this guiding spirit was not a *personal* being, but a *neuter*. Nor can we say what the *δαιμόνιον* was. Some think it was the conscience; some the practical instinct; others the indirect tact. But we believe he refers it to the supernatural. Theologians say he had a view of the Spirit.

Whatever it was, it had two aspects. It was without and divine, and it was addressed to something within.

He believed in divinations and dreams. He speaks of gods and their attributes, and, no doubt, did believe that he was under the guidance of Divine Providence. As to his actual belief in God, he entirely separated himself from superstitious views. He did not hold to the fables of old. He was both a polytheist and a theist. He believed in a multitude of gods, or else he was a most wicked hypocrite; yet, while it was clear that he believed in "gods many and lords many," still he believed in one ruling all. He wanted the people of Athens to believe that he worshipped Apollo and all others; but while he believed all this, and did it, he had a conviction of one God, high and superior to all others.

2. The *nature* of *virtue*. He may be regarded as the founder of Ethics. He was the first who inquired into the nature of good and evil; still he inquired into the nature of them only in a speculative manner. He is distinguished from all the Pre-Socratic school by this: that all his discussions turned on *duty*. He could not conceive how a man should know the good and yet not do it. It was to him a logical contradiction that the man who sought his own well-being should knowingly neglect it. He identified virtue with wisdom. His system of religion dwelt especially on justice, temperance, and fortitude. All virtues were combined in wisdom (*σοφία*). Can virtue be taught?

was a question discussed by him and the Sophists. He denied it; *σοφία* was a thing that could not be taught. He referred it to God. It is in Him alone.

Now as to some points disputed about Socrates. For example, was he a Utilitarian? We do not think he was. It does not agree in all respects with Utilitarianism. He showed that virtue always led to felicity, (*εὐδαιμονία*), which means blessedness, rather than happiness or pleasure.

He supposed that knowledge was connected with a pre-existing state, which in the change from that state to the present had escaped the memory, and only needed a philosopher to call it forth. He said that man had lost his former knowledge, yet there was power in the mind to re-kindle it again. He thought there was a place and time of judgment and retribution. He believed in the immortality of the soul. He left out the doctrine of the will, which was first brought in by Aristotle. "If a man is wise he *will* be virtuous."

Next, what was his belief as to the immortality of the soul? His view as to what it was, was very dark and vague. He felt sure that the soul would live after death, in a certain state, but he could not tell what that state would be. He thought that he would be blessed. When asked by his friends what they should do with him when he was dead, he answered: "Just what you please, if you can only catch me."

Next we view his trial.

C.—Grounds of Accusation.

1. *That he neglected the worship of the gods.* This was not true. He did worship the gods, and in the purest manner he knew how. It may, however, have thus been somewhat different from the general worship performed by the people.

2. *That he introduced new gods.* He accounted for things differently from the people. It is true that he worshipped one God, which was a new feature.

3. *That he corrupted the morals of the youth*: By bringing in of new customs and of a new mode of culture and education. This charge was not well founded. He may have undermined some theories, but he really taught high morals.

[illegible]

[illegible]

[illegible]

[illegible]

[illegible]

[illegible]

attention.

[illegible]

He died a martyr. He might have escaped his fate by bribery or by paying a fine, but he scorned the idea of fleeing and breaking the laws of the state. Meletus, Anytus, and Lycon accused him. He fully answered the first charge. He had heartily worshipped the gods of Athens, although a theist. As to the second charge, he could have denied it; δαιμόνιον was but a higher idea of the general idea of God. As to corruption of youth, what was the corruption? He was pure. He defied his accusers, and so died. All early systems look to him; all following flow out from him. He was the isthmus between the two.

He had a wide influence in his day. The youth eagerly gathered around him. Xenophon was an admirer of Socrates and became his biographer, though not properly a philosopher.

We have now to make some closing remarks on the scattered schools. We consider

I. Their excellencies.

1. They awakened thought. It was already coming to the surface, but they promoted its growth. Then one school did not sway the other, and this characteristic has continued down to the present time. The "Intermediate School" might, however, owe something to those which went before.

2. They anticipated truths. These truths were mingled with error, but they were, nevertheless, started at this time. The Ionians taught that there were elements: the Pythagoreans showed that there was some form which subordinated the whole; hence arose morphology: the Eleatics brought out the existence of the unchangeable. Anaxagoras noticed the νοῦς and the doctrine of chemical affinity; and Democritus was the author of the Atomic theory, which is held to this day.

II. Their defects.

1. Their method was empirical. They gathered a few facts and rose to a general law. It was not complete enough for induction.

Whewell calls it the decomposition of facts.

It forms an essential part of induction, but taken alone is a mere exercise of thought and gives no result.

2. Their defective ethical views.

In none of these schools was there an ethical science. The best the Pythagoreans could do was to describe it as a square number. Socrates was the father of Ethics.

Several schools ramified from Socrates, but Plato was his greatest pupil.

There are several schools claiming origin from Socrates. Of his followers we notice,

1. Xenophon, a soldier and scholar, the biographer o Socrates. There is a discrepancy between his and Plato's accounts of Socrates. Probably all that Xenophon says of him is true, while Plato undoubtedly put many of his own opinions in Socrates' mouth. Then this apparent discrepancy is also largely due to the fact that they looked at Socrates from different standpoints. Xenophon was not a philosopher like Plato.

2. Euclid (not the great mathematician) of Megara, who was the founder of the Megaric, or Dialectic school. This school took up the dialectic side of Socrates' character, mixing his speculations with that of Parmenides: thus giving, as it were, a new edition of the Eleatic doctrine.

3. Aristippus of Cyrene, a colonial city in Africa, whose school was, therefore, called Cyrenaic. He said that *pleasure* was the greatest good. The system was, if anything, Protagorean. Hence the Epicureans. It led to sensuality. These were called the " Moral Schools."

4. Antisthenes, who founded the school called Cynic, whence the Stoic school. His doctrince was that *virtue* is the only good. Pain is not evil. It led to the Pharisaic school—Diogenes.

These schools sprang from the professed followers of Socrates. But all were thrown in the shade by that complete Socratist—

B.—Plato.

Plato, the son of Aristo, was born 429 B. C. At the age of twenty he became a hearer of Socrates, by whose advice

he attached himself to the study of philosophy, and continued with him until Socrates' death. Then he left Athens and went to Megara. He is supposed to have traveled very extensively for ten years or more. He visited Cyrene, Egypt, Sicily, Phœnicia and, as we have reason to suppose, Magna Græcia. In this last place he became acquainted with Pythagorean philosophy, which was then in its "highest bloom." After these ten years spent in travel, in the year 389 or 388 B. C. he returned to Athens and taught philosophy outside of the city in the famous garden of the Academy. Here he expounded his doctrines to all who visited him.

There has been much speculation as to whence he derived his philosophy. The following account has been given of the various sources. Thirty or forty works are attributed to him, but some perhaps are spurious. Twenty or thirty generally are acknowledged. Grote believes that most works attributed to him are genuine. His letters are probably spurious. He got his Ethics from Socrates, many of his views from Heraclitus, his Pythagoreanism from Archytas. Parmenides and Hermogenes, his instructor, taught him the Eleatic doctrine; his method of discussion he adopted from Zeno; while his irony and doubt on dark subjects came from Socrates. To this we must add the many ideas which his travels gave him, as for instance, transmigration, which he derived from the East.

He may be said to have united two philosophies, to have combined ideas and things, the constant "flux" of Heraclitus and the unity of Parmenides, with the order (*κόσμος*) of the Pythagoreans. He admired the Pythagorean theory and also the "flux" theory. He enters between the two systems and endeavors to harmonize them. His was an original but not an independent mind. He combined all his elements "ideas," "things," etc., in the one great "idea," (*εἶδος*) and (*ἰδέα*,) using the latter term for deep subjects. His great doctrine is, there is one *ἰδέα* in the Divine Mind, *i. e.*, something that is supersensual and supernatural, above all human things, but below all divine things. Whether it was a creation or was independent of the Divine Mind is unsettled. But it was before the mind of God, and the grandest thing before it. Man once had knowledge of this idea, but had lost it by sin; hence, he believed in an original state of purity, a fall, and a state of sin. The contemplation of this idea was, he said, the highest exercise of the soul.

His philosophy may best be considered under three heads:

1. His Dialectics, (mode of inquiry.) 2. His Physics, (what things are.) 3. His Ethics, (what things ought to be.) These are mixed together in his dialogues, and some have attempted to discover what treatises he wrote first, what last, and what before he left Athens; but these attempts have largely failed. His chief method was the Dialectic. Many suppose his first work was the Phædrus. That it was the earliest, however, cannot be proved from any internal evidence. His book on Laws was probably the latest. The titles of his works are:

On Dialectics.	On Physics.	On Ethics.
Theætetus.	Timæus.	Phædrus.
Cratylus.	(Spurious.)	Republic and Laws.
Gorgias.	Minos and Hipparchus.	The Banquet.
Protagoras.		Hippias.
Parmenides.	Letters.	Philebus.
The Sophist.		Virtue.

There are a great many spurious works ascribed to him.

The Platonic Dialectics, a phrase from his Eleatic speculative philosophy, is much the same as what we now understand by "speculative philosophy." It was all arranged around the "true and good" and "essential being." He constantly distinguishes between δόξα and ἐπιστήμη. The latter means highest wisdom, and lies in the mind like seed in the ground. This wisdom cannot be reached except by thinking, by abstraction and by mathematical training. Δόξα means things that might or might not be; it is the possible. All physical speculation depends on probability. He illustrates all this by the famous example of a cave. In the front of the cave moved a number of figures; within was man chained with his back to the light; the figures pass before the cave, but he cannot turn and see them; he can see only their shadows. To a knowledge of the figures themselves, we must arrive by a higher νοῦς.

There are two great works written in modern times upon the Platonic philosophy.

The first is that of Archer Butler, entitled "The History of Greek Philosophy." His first volume is not of much value, but when he comes to speak of Plato, he enters freely into the spirit of his work. His exposition of the ideal theory, in particular, is the finest ever drawn. Butler here mixes some of his own high thought with that of Plato, so that we are not quite sure that Plato is entitled to all he gets. Butler had a Platonic mind of the highest order, and hence his ability to appreciate thoroughly the lofty ideas of Plato.

The second is the work of Grote, entitled "Plato and his Contemporaries." He takes an entirely different side of the question as to Plato's character, and this side of the question he has thoroughly appreciated. He does not seem at all capable, however, of contemplating Plato.

There are two sides to the mind of Plato—

1. As seen in his search for truth, his attempts to set aside error, and his employment of the Socratic irony. He puts a series of questions, and shows by asking "Is truth this, or is it that?" that we have not yet reached truth, and at the close, instead of showing what is not truth and what is truth, he shows that it is impossible to reach truth.

2. The positive side of Plato's mind, by which he seeks to establish positive truth; (well developed by Butler.)

We cannot understand the philosophy of Plato without understanding his ideal theory. It is not the same as the modern ideal theory of sense perception. Let us put ourselves in his position, and try to appreciate his surroundings. He was in the midst of a varied class of thinkers, some of whom held that all things had been from all eternity, and would go on to all eternity; others that all things were fixed, and there could be no change. These culminated in Heraclitus, who said that there could be no immutability. The senses cannot give us the true being. Again, he turned to others, and found them holding that things never change, and that all change was, not in our minds, but in our senses. There might seem to be changes, but they were on the surface of things which never themselves changed. Now, how could he reconcile these? He thought he would find a reconciliation in the Pythagorean school, which taught that number would harmonize all. But this view, says Plato, is a mystery; and so out of this chaos arose Plato's ideal theory. He employs the word *εἶδος* and *ἰδέα* instead of numbers, the word used by Pythagoras.

Now let us consider the Dialectics or discussion of the idea of Plato. We have given (*a*) general notice of the idea, and (*b*) we proceed to consider it as related—

1. To the Divine Mind.
2. To the Human Mind.
3. To the Physical World.

1. What relation does it bear to the Divine Mind? Plato was a polytheist, but like his great master, he too rose to the conception of one God. If you had asked Plato what the idea of the Divine Mind or the Divine Nature was, he would have said that it was the very essence of the Divine Mind; that it had been in the Divine Mind from eternity, the model which it had before itself. Again, there are passages in which he seems to make it independent of the Divine Mind. Plato could not reconcile these two views. If one asks whether virtue is a creation of the Divine Mind or independent of it, no answer can be given. We must, therefore, take the view as he gives it—that there is a God and an idea. He developed a doctrine akin to the doctrine of the Trinity, but not that of the Christian church. Whether this idea of the Unity and Trinity originated in some of the eastern nations or with himself is not certain. It is certain that he had the idea of an essential God, and along with it the idea which is connected with God. He had some idea like that of the Trinity. He said there was—

(1.) A God.
(2.) A *λόγος* (same as developed by St. John.)
(3.) A manifestation of the excellence of the idea.

Again, he held that this idea became manifested by God in nature. Along with this Deity he had an idea of matter not created by God, but existing coeval with God, and thus matter was passive as opposed to active;—not the same as "matter" now, but matter capable of receiving the impress of God—over which God had no absolute power, for he

This idea was [illegible]
[illegible]
[illegible]
[illegible]
[illegible]
[illegible]
[illegible]

conceives the possibility that matter might offer opposition to the formative energy of ideas, and gives intimation of the presence in the world of a principle in nature hostile to God.

There was, in addition, a soul of the world, which is intermediate between God and the world. This soul was the only thing that God had created; then it created gods, demons, men, and the world out of matter.

Plato, in the Timæus makes the sensible world to be formed by a creator, after the pattern of an idea; but in this he lays down as a condition that this creator (*δημιουργός*) should find at hand a something which was apt to receive and exhibit this ideal image. This something Plato compares to the matter which is fashioned by the artisan; whence the name *ὕλη*.

As to the doctrine of the origin of things, he held that God was caused and evil uncaused. Evil did not and could not proceed from God. He says evil comes from two sources:

a. From the soul of the world. There was a limitation to the power of the soul of the world. This limited being gave rise to limited things, which were therefore imperfect.

b. To the incapacity of matter, of *ὕμη*. The soul could not fashion this matter into beauty and perfection, because it was incapable of these qualities. Divine goodness he held to be the final cause of the universe, divine energy the efficient, and ideas the formal.

2. What relation does it bear to the human mind? He held that the human mind had passed through a number of forms, (like the doctrine of metempsychosis), and believed in a previous state of existence, a state of perfection and a subsequent fall. A soul addicted to lust and animal passions had formerly been in lower animals. It is true, then, in a certain sense, that Plato believed in a previous state. He described the world as independent of God. He held that every man had, in the depths of his nature, a pure state of soul, but it had been lost to him in his degeneration, and existed, therefore, in an imperfect form. The way of reclaiming and rescuing it was by abstraction, especially by the study of mathematics and geometry, and

still better by dialectics. These, he said, trained the intellect, and as men's reason had been degraded and overwhelmed by the body, it was the greatest achievement of the mind to rise to the contemplation of the good, the true and the beautiful. Therefore all the spirit of his researches and his dialectics was to train the mind to rise to the conception of these ideas. On this account he put a series of questions to a slave, to show that by education a slave even could be raised from a low state. He taught that all education should thus elevate men by means of philosophical and not by physical speculations. This is its grand end. The *νοῦς* or *λόγος* makes man partake of the Divine being, and by it we are all to rise and contemplate the eternal pattern. Matter with him was co-eternal with God. The soul apprehends the idea as essentially the same with itself. He proves that—

(1) There is a connection between soul and ideas, from their homogeneity.
(2) This is attested by the longing of the soul for perfection.
(3) It is for the philosopher to make abstractions from the senses after the image of the ideas.
(4) The soul is as eternal as the ideas.

3. What relation does it sustain to the phenomenal world? His answer was:

(1) As many to one.
(2) As single to opposite.
(3) Simple to confused.
(4) Indivisible to divisible.
(5) Unchangeable to changeable.
(6) Divine to necessary.
(7) Absolute to the relative.
(8) Exemplar to copy.
(9) Good to display of goods.
(10) Object of science to object of opinion.
(11) Original to participant.

The sensible world was to him an important image of the ideal. The idea stood to it in the relation of a pattern or model. He employed several phrases to denote it, viz., the relation between the idea and the external world, such as *ἀφαίρεσις* or abstraction, *μέθεξις*, communication or parti-

cipation, and παράδειγμα, pattern, plan, or model. The state of the external world was, that the soul of the world was continually creating new things, and these things participated in the imperfections of the matter from which they sprang. The great object was to elevate men to the contemplation of this idea. He said that every object around us had a participation in the idea. The more of this idea that thing contained, the more perfect it was. Love was highest and contained much of this idea. The Platonic love consisted in seeing the idea in a beautiful man or woman. Beauty was an embodiment of the Divine Mind. The Platonic beauty consistsin a participation in this idea; a thing is more beautiful because it has a clearer mold given it by the idea. Beauty, especially when immaterial, was contemplated by the λόγος. Material beauty consisted in exact proportion and adjustment.

Virtue was the love of the idea and of God, as embodied in it. Socrates would have said it consisted in the performance of active duties, but Plato sought the idea in everything.

We have said that his philosophy may be divided into Dialectics or Logic, Physics and Ethics.

Physics means what exists and is.

Logic means how to reach an Idea of it, and gives us the nature of the idea.

Ethics means what ought to be.

We will now consider

The Platonic Physics.

Plato applied himself with much less zeal to physical investigations than to those of an ethical or dialectical character. Only in one dialogue, the Timæus, do we find any extended evolution of physical doctrines. Plato conceives the world as the image of the good; as the work of the Divine munificence.

According to the above division of his philosophy, Psychology would come under Physics. It is not fully developed. In all the schools we have some Psychology. In the Eleatic school we have a distinction between αἴσθησις and λόγος, and the δόξα, or region of probable truth.

We have a threefold division of Plato's theory of knowledge, that is, of the faculties.

Psychological Divisions.

αἴσθησις.	Animal love.	*εἰκασία.*
δόξα.	*θύμος.*	*διάνοια* (*πίστις.*)
νοῦς or *λόγος.*	Love.	*νόησις.*

Explanation of the Table.

The first column would be our *cognitive* powers. *Αἴσθησις*, sensation; *δόξα*, notions intermediate between ideas and sensations; *νοῦς*, (*λόγος*), idea. The philosophers of the day reckoned Physics as the region of the doubtful, and classed it under the *δόξα*, and above this, Plato places the *νοῦς*.

The second column corresponds to our motive powers of mind. Animal love (*ἐπιθυμητικόν*) corresponds to what we call the active powers; love, to the highest of all, and means love in the absolute: while *θυμός*, called "anger," was, in truth, the impulsive power of the mind.

In the third column, *εἰκασία*, the region of shadows and unrealities, where things have one form to-day and another to-morrow; *διάνοια*, the region of discursive thought, *i. e.*, the faculty by which from something given, we reach conclusions; *νόησις*, the region where we live in realities.

He believed in the immortality of the soul for four reasons:

1. Because of its pre-existence. He believed the soul had existed previously, and, therefore, would exist hereafter.
2. The second argument was drawn from the fact that soul has a different life from matter.
3. The simplicity of the soul argues its immortality. The body may be separated into its constituents; the soul is simple and indivisible, and consequently immortal.
4. The doctrine of contraries implies it. Life implies death, and death, life.

[illegible]
[illegible] Hess [illegible]
[illegible]
[illegible] the [illegible].

[illegible]
[illegible]
[illegible]
[illegible]

[illegible] Baltimore [illegible]
[illegible]

[illegible]
[illegible]
un [illegible]
[illegible] κακός
[illegible] in [illegible] ile [illegible]
[illegible]
[illegible]

[illegible] vel [illegible] in
[illegible] et [illegible]
[illegible]

The Platonic Ethics.

He drew his views from Socrates. Under this head he includes Æsthetics and Politics, which are discussed in the Greater Hippias, Phædrus, Banquet, Philebus, and in the 7th book of the Republic. With him Ethics proper consisted in the contemplation of the one, the good. Φρόνησις (wisdom) was the highest virtue to him. Under this he placed fortitude, temperance, and justice, the cardinal virtues. Socrates made virtue consist in a voluntary intellectual act. Some have supposed the voluntary element comes in Plato's Ethics, but it is vaguely, if at all. Socrates held that no man was willingly wicked. Aristotle also gives a place to will in moral good and evil. Socrates said that virtue must be a gift of God, and could not be learned. Plato tries to show how it may be reached by abstraction, and from this he rises to one God, whom he makes the idea of good. The highest exercise of the soul, said he, is that in which we contemplate the good of God.

He divided his Ethics into: 1. Æsthetics. 2. Politics.

1. Æsthetics. He is the first that regarded Æsthetics as an art. He discussed the subject of beauty. There was a lower beauty, he said, which could be seen by the senses, and a higher beauty which could be seen by the πίστις. But the highest beauty could be perceived only by the νοῦς. He made beauty to consist in the possession of the idea by the object; and things are beautiful only as they partake of this divine idea. If man degraded it there could be no beauty. Our aim, therefore, should be to train it, and thus to rise to a contemplation of beauty.

Thus the Platonic *Eros* is the contemplation of the idea in the object, or the desire to behold it, the highest exercise of the mind was the contemplation of *κάλλος* and *τὸ ἀγαθόν*. According to him beauty was communicated to the soul of the universe by limiting it, *e. g.*, a right-angled isosceles triangle, and other figures were emblems of beauty.

The virtue of Plato does not consist in pleasure (ἡδονή), but,

1. In participation in the Idea which was originally given to us.

2. It must be realized in affection, in actuality.

3. It required reason and intelligence.

4. It must cultivate itself by practicing Science and the Arts.

5. Pure and painless pleasure might enter into it.

If we combine these we get the doctrine of virtue, according to Plato.

All this was very intimately connected with his Æsthetics.

2. Politics. He describes in his *πολιτεία* an ideal republic. This is represented as consisting of three classes of men. The highest were rulers; and the next, also, though under these, ruled to some extent; the third was in a state of hopeless degradation. His government, then, is an aristocratic one, but an aristocracy of intellect. This was only an ideal government which never did exist, nor could nor should have existed. He has another political treatise called the "Laws." In this he pictures a different commonwealth. In the "Laws" marriage is to be obeyed. In the "Republic" he abolishes the institution of marriage, and opposes the living in pairs.

Plato gives us an ideal picture of a commonwealth. He did not, however, mingle in the active affairs of political life. He gives us in his Republic, his idea of a perfect government. In his law treatise he laid down certain laws which he thought should be recognized; in the latter he tells how to live under the existing state.

There is thus an inconsistency between his Republic, on the one hand, and the Laws on the other. The common way of reconciling these is, that in the former he tells us what ought to be, but in the latter how to act, and what to do. The grand feature of the Platonic state is the exclusive sacrifice of the individual to the state, the reference of moral to political virtue. In a perfect state, all things, joy, sorrow, and even eyes and hands, must be common to all; that the social life may be, as it were, the life of the individual man. (See Schwegler, page 104.)

He divided the people into three classes:

1. *Χρηματισταί.*—The ignorant men or the artisans. This must mean the masses, who were subject both to the councillors and rulers. He had no idea that all could be raised to the highest standard.

2. *'Επικουρικόν.*—The executive class, or military rulers under the chief advisers.

3. *Βουλευτικόν.*—The counselors, or intellectual, *i. e.*, the aristocracy.

Placing these opposite the divisions in the above table, we have three classes or ranks: that of the ruler corresponding to the reason, that of the watcher or warrior answering to spirit, and that of craftsman, which is made parallel to the appetites or sensuous desires. To these three ranks belong three separate functions: to the first, that of making law, and caring for the general good; to the second, that of defending the public welfare from the attacks of external foes; to the third, the care of separate interests and wants, as agriculture, mechanics, etc. From each of these three ranks and its functions the state derives a peculiar virtue, viz.: wisdom, from the ruler; virtue, from the warrior; and temperance, from the craftsman, so far as he lives in obedience to his rulers.

In summing up the philosophy of Plato, let us enumerate his excellencies and defects.

His Excellencies.

1. His style. He is called "Homerus Philosophorum." We have found no such writer in ancient or modern times. Thucydides, the model historian, resembles, but cannot equal him. Cicero is not so elevated; nor do any of the great poets equal him. Plato proposes to banish poetry from his Republic, as tending to influence the passions, but he does not banish it from his own writings. Plato descends with dignity from the greatest heights to the lowest familiarities.

2. His mental qualities. He embodies a wonderful comprehensiveness with remarkable acuteness. We have some minds as acute, but none combine the two in such harmony. He comes down to answer an opponent, and tears his argument to pieces, and a moment after rises into the most lofty speculations. His ideal theory is an example of the comprehensiveness of his intellect. His analysis of the opinions of others illustrates his great acuteness.

3. The great and noble truths in his system. These are seen:

a. In his Dialectics. (1.) He says there was an idea before the Divine mind, and (2) that this idea was wrought out in nature. Each plant assumes a particular form, and so every leaf. Every branch leaves the parent stock at a typical angle. (3.) Thus there is a law, and all these typical forms are under law, and man can discover this law. Now, we say it is in the office of science to discover this law of order. The difference between the modern and the Platonic science is that Plato thought this law could be discovered by looking into the mind. Francis Bacon shows that that cannot be. He says that we must reach it by careful observation of particulars, and from these rise to laws and forms. Man is not the *magister*, but the *minister* of nature. Bacon's end was the same, but his means were widely different. Even as there is an idea in nature, so in the human mind; and man can rise to true forms translated from the *ἰδέα* of Plato. These ideas in the mind are fundamental principles underlying belief.

b. In his views of beauty, which were higher than those of many modern philosophers. He is the father of the Æsthetic science of his day. He connects beauty with the Divine nature. He and Socrates were constantly seeking the essential being. He would say, "God is shadowed forth in his works." He calls things without beauty *τά ἄπειρα*, "things without form." But when the idea comes upon a thing it becomes beautiful. Beauty thus is gaining something out of the waste, and putting an idea and harmony upon it by means of the idea. Beauty consists in proportion and adjustments. He says the beauty of certain triangles consists in all the elements of formative power, and in all the harmony of parts. This contains an immense amount of truth, and, in later times, became a favorite theory. As there is an objective beauty in the world around us, there is also a subjective taste which may be brought forth and cultivated.

c. In his Ethics. (1.) He traces the morally good to an eternal reality, (2.) and connects it with the Divine nature. It is a heavenly gift and being lost is capable of being restored. (3.) He says, but not in the same sense that Moses said it, that man was created in the image of God, and therefore could discern between good and evil; he does

[illegible]

[illegible]

[illegible]

not deny the doctrine of conscience. (4.) H› acknowledges a fall and an opposing principle in man's nature, which he represents by the illustration of two steeds harnessed to a chariot; one of which goes straight forward, but the other is constantly flying off. Plato places beauty on a level with morality.

His Defects.

1. Lack of system, and an exuberance of theories and fancies. By far the finest exposition of these theories is given us by Archer Butler, who seems sometimes to mix his own views with those of Plato. A different view is given by Grote, whose object was to show that there were inconsistencies in Plato's philosophy; but, being reared in the school of Comte, he could not appreciate that philosophy. Leibnitz has the same difficulty. No one has yet fully evolved Plato's system; perhaps Plato himself could not have systematized his own mind. We cannot get at his ideal theory.

2. Defects in his method; it is analytic rather than inductive. It is often said that Socrates and Plato proceeded by the inductive method, but this is a mistake. They did, no doubt, look to facts, but only as examples. They took first a phenomenon, and tried to explain it; they said, "Let us inquire what it is. Is it this or is it that?" Then they got some idea and looked to facts as examples. For instance, they saw a beautiful statue and inquired, "What is beauty?" Thus they obtained a rude idea, and traced it to the Divine mind. They found "God manifested in his works." Bacon, on the contrary, collected facts, and let these facts suggest the law.

3. Mysticism in his expositions and errors in his views. This is seen—

a. Dialectics. As to his ideal theory. What this is, is a disputed point, and ever will be. It is like a magnificent cloud tinged with the bright rays of the sun; appearing now distant, nearer, ever shifting, ever changing. It is not, however, to be regarded as independent of God. This idea is to be found everywhere; as Plato says, "in the very dust of the earth." In modern times the microscope confirms it in beautiful crystalline forms, which it reveals. So this idea pervades the air, for it, too, is full of germs of animate being, ready to spring into life when put in favorable circumstances. But whatever this idea is, Plato did not see how to obtain it, or how we were to rise to the contemplation of God. Aristotle blames him for placing the idea above things instead of in things. We fail to understand the objection. There is no idea independent of particulars; but is gathered from singulars by induction.

b. Ethics. (1.) As to Beauty. There is no general beauty after all. It is a quality in objects. He thought by contemplating an object of beauty, he could rise to its abstract idea. Beauty is not an abstraction, but is after all in the body, in the forms and colors. He looked at beauty merely in the abstract. This error was corrected by Aristotle. Besides he placed beauty as high as good.

(2.) As to Morality. In this respect he errs.

a. In making the highest exercise of the soul to consist in the contemplation of the good, whereas it consists in the contemplation of the Good Being. This led to Neo-Platonism, and they called this state of abstraction ecstacy. This error did not appear until later.

b. He had not sufficiently deep views of sin as voluntary. This applies to Socrates, who said that good was a form of intelligence. Plato had a view of some primitive sin. But while he had a view of a fall from some higher state, he did not have the true idea of sin as its cause. He identified it with metempsychosis.

c. He does not see the way to elevate the mass of mankind. " To the poor the Gospel is preached." With Plato it was only the few to whom it was to be preached, the poor not included. He had selected a few whom he would elevate; there was no idea of elevating the masses. His was a system of intellectual oligarchy. Plato was an intellectual aristocrat. How different from the doctrines which Paul presented in the same city! Plato taught that men were unequal; Paul that they were equal before God.

d. His commonwealth was utterly impracticable. His system was ideal and Utopian; it has never been put in practice. There is no liberty of thought or of action in it. This *de legibus* is a mere theoretical treatise. Such a com-

monwealth as his is to be ruled by men who had obtained the highest excellence in philosophy by contemplating the Grand Exemplar. Such rulers the people would not have trusted, for the rulers would undertake what the masses would not. In fact his whole theory never should be put in practice, for—

e. His whole system of government was an intellectual oligarchy, which took away man's freedom and did not allow every man to think for himself.

f. He permited in his Republic a promiscuous intercourse of the sexes. He did not favor marriages. A man was not to love or even to know his parents, for that would make him weak and effeminate. He did not see that the family relation was a part of God's plan. There was, however, no sensualism, or what is known as "free love," in his system.

g. In his writings are many immoral passages; as bad as any Byron or Shakespeare have written, and such as no Christian writer of the present day would pen.

C.—Aristotle.

Aristotle, (384–322 B. C.,) was born at Stagira, a seaport in Chalcidice. His father, who claimed descent from Æsculapius, was a physician and friend of the king of Macedonia. He became a disciple of Plato at the age of eighteen, and was the most illustrious of his scholars, being called by him his "thinker." He had no tendency to admire praise, or to agree with any one, but was of a carping spirit. He had more sagacity, and less of the ideal tendency, than his master. His speculations differed from Plato's; yet some passages in Plato seem to have given rise to some of his thoughts. After the death of his master he went to Hermo, in Mysia, thence to the court of Philip, where for ten years he was tutor of Alexander. He afterwards went to Athens, where he taught in the Lyceum. He is charged with atheism, his god being a metaphysical deity. Leaving Athens he went to Chalcis, where he died. The minds of Plato and Aristotle were of a different order. Each was typical, and it is said by the Germans that all minds are either of a Platonic or Aristotelian order. This assertion is rather surprising, but full of truth. Plato is running over with theories. He made a general view of things a grand view, whether accurate or not. He was speculative and theoretical. Aristotle was especially gifted with the discursive faculty; he is eminently practical, and many of his theories are in anticipation of modern philosophy. The one was the imitator of the ancient, the other the type of the present. Aristotle sought to be accurate; Plato to get general truths. Plato would run a thing up to a certain point with great acuteness, and then he would break off and leave his pupils befogged in mysticism. Aristotle would not be satisfied, but would try to go further. For example: As to his view of memory. Plato says it is to be accounted for by the doctrine of metempsychosis. "No," says Aristotle, "but by the laws of association, by contiguity and contrast."

Aristotle was great in all branches. He founded many and expounded many more. Ethics was founded by Socrates; Political Science by Plato; Natural History by Aristotle. He founded, also, Historical Criticism and Logic, at least the name did not exist before him. He did not found Metaphysics, but one of his most important treatises is written upon it. He was the founder of Psychology; true, it existed before him in a very rude state, but he first endeavored to give a full analysis of the faculties of the mind. His sole aim was not to speculate, but to arrive at accuracy.

THE PHILOSOPHY OF ARISTOTLE.—PERIPATETIC.

He was a pupil of Plato, yet differed widely from his master. It was the tendency of his mind to differ from others. He said he respected Plato, but truth much more. He is characterized by categorical opinions, and he endeavored to establish them by subtle arguments. Plato was not willing to submit his theories to any accurate tests, while Aristotle was anxious to test everything, and to express the truth accurately. Aristotle had a nomenclature peculiar to himself. His philosophy is contained very largely in his phraseology; he uses the same phrases in all his works.

[illegible] [illegible]
[illegible] [illegible]

It appeals [illegible]
[illegible] [illegible]
the [illegible]
[illegible]
[illegible] [illegible]
[illegible]
[illegible] [illegible]
[illegible] [illegible]

We will not, in this place, dwell on his physical investigations, but will confine ourselves to his philosophy.

His philosophy comes under three heads.

1. Logic=the search after truth.
2. Ethics= " for what ought to be.
3. Physics= " " is.

He made a distinction between the sciences which are theoretical and practical. The distinction is not the same as that between science and art. (Hamilton doubts whether this distinction has been correctly drawn by Whately.)

We begin our review of his philosophy by looking at

His Metaphysics.

He had a treatise on this subject which passes under his name, but is not so called by himself. The phrase τὰ μετὰ τὰ φυσικά is supposed to have been used by one of his annotators, Andronicus. It relates to subjects beyond Physics. The name he gives it is "First Philosophy," a happy phrase, because he assigns to it a special field of inquiry into "first truths," that is, truths which have their faith in themselves. It is the deepest of sciences, and the last reached.

We must first know the other sciences, as developed before we come to it. According to him his "First Philosophy" treats of being.

He argues, if there be an eternal substance, then Physics would be first; but if there be an immaterial and eternal essence, which is the ground of all being, then must there be an antecedent and universal philosophy. But when he is inquiring into entity, he is in reality inquiring into causes.

Method of Writing. Introduced the logical processes of Division and Definition (used by Socrates). He begins with these, and then gives historical and critical sketches of eminent philosophers writing about the same matter. Lastly, he unfolds his own views.

Distinctions. *a.* Between ὕλη and εἶδος, matter and form. Matter is independent of God. Upon the ὕλη God placed the εἶδος, which latter in all movement is the logical principle.

b. Between causes.

There are four causes of Aristotle in inquiring into entity.

The word "cause" is used vaguely by him; more so than in modern times.

A cause now is understood as all that is necessary to account for and explain a phenomenon. Aristotle's causes were,

1. Material—ἐξ οὗ (τὴν ὕλην καὶ τὸ ὑποκείμενον.)
2. Formal—καθ' ὃ (τὴν οὐσίαν καὶ τὸ τί ἦν εἶναι.)
3. Efficient—ὑφ' οὗ (ὅθεν ἡ ἀρχὴ τῆς κινήσεως.)
4. Final—δι' ὃ (τὸ οὗ ἕνεκεν καὶ τὸ ἀγαθόν.)

These causes were universally received for about one thousand years.

He illustrates his meaning by a statue. Suppose it in the temple of Hercules, in a niche. He inquires:

1. What was the matter out of which it was formed? It is marble. This, then, is the material cause. The same may be established in regard to anything else, as trees, etc.

2. What is its form? It is a demi-god. That is the formal cause.

3. What is the efficient cause? The hammer and chisel of the sculptor.

4. What was the final cause? On account of what was it formed? To adorn this niche in the temple.

Now this same thing he finds in nature. Look at a tree. The material cause is the matter which it draws from the ground and atmosphere; but it has a form peculiar to itself; this is the formal. The efficient cause is the chemical and vital power; its final cause or purpose is to raise an idea of beauty in our minds, to give shade and fruit. Everything, in short, has these four causes.

c. Between attributes in the universe.

1. Δύναμις, "capacity." "Power" is too strong a word, as we shall see. This is allied to the formal cause; like the statue in the block of marble; it is there in the quarry, but in the state of δύναμις.

2. It comes forth into ἐνέργεια or "activity." Intermediate between these two there is a third phrase.

3. Εντελέχεια; readiness to act. When I hold a piece of chalk in my hand it has δύναμις to fall to the ground; when it falls it is ἐνέργεια; when on the point of falling,

[illegible]

[illegible] ambiguous [illegible]

[illegible]

[illegible]

[illegible] only [illegible]

(1) [illegible] allude [illegible]

[illegible]

2 [illegible]

[illegible] drilling [illegible]

[illegible]

[illegible]

[illegible]

[illegible]

[illegible]

[illegible]

between the time of withdrawing the hand and the time of falling, there is ἐντελέχεια. Here is the doctrine of the conservation of forces. Coal has the capacity to give heat, a δύναμις; when just tumbling into the fire it has ἐνέργεια. There is thus a potential and and an actual energy in forces. When this potentiality comes forth into actuality, it is ἐνέργεια. When ready to act, ἐντελέχεια. The result of the three is ἔργα, works; that is the completed deed; a fixed tendency or ἕξις is the result of an ενέργεια.

Example of a watch spring:

Δύναμις is steel unformed.

'Ενέργεια is formed spring working.

'Εντελέχεια is formed spring not working.

"Εργα are works.

"Εξις is habit, tendency to go.

He anticipated modern philosophy and science, but certainly he has set forth some things on this point that have since been proved.

There is a distinction between ὅτι and διότι. The one, ὅτι, inquires what a thing is, the other, διότι, how it is. The latter inquires into causes.

He had a distinction, also, as to priority. When one thing is prior to another it is in five respects, namely, time, nature, arrangement, dignity, and causation. So much for his metaphysics.

His Psychology.

He has a treatise on the ψυχή, or vital principle. Not what we mean by the soul; plants and animals have a ψυχή in this respect. He begins with an inquiry as to what genus to refer it. Is soul a substance, quality, or quantity? Are all souls of the same species? He then examines the theory of atoms, in the discussion of which he treats Democritus with great respect. "Everything was formed from atoms, and all comes to one soul." He was, then, a materialist. He defines ψυχή as "the first ἐντελέχεια of a natural, organic body, which body has life potentially"—in δύναμις.

He says better, "It is that by which we live, feel, and reason." Notice his peculiar phraseology, which would be unintelligible did we not understand his peculiarities. A body having life in δύναμις, it comes forth in ἐντελέχεια, and thus is ψυχή. He says the soul is not separate from the body, but is an act of the body. The soul is not mere matter, but both a λογος and an εἶδος. It has the three higher causes, leaving out the δύναμις. It has several qualities.

1st. The Nutritive power. The division of the faculties of the soul are regulated according to the division of living creatures. The nutritive faculty, the property of vegetables, and sensation, the property of animals, are steps to the development of the human soul. The soul itself is nothing other than the union of the different activities of an organic body in one common end. He gave the first arrangement of the faculties of the mind.

2d. The Sensitive Power, αἴσθησις. The proper objects of sense are two—

(1) Those apprehended by one sense.

(2) Those apprehended by more or all.

This is also the distinction between "proper percepts," *i. e.*, by one sense; and "common percepts," by more than one. This is the modern distinction between primary and secondary qualities of matter brought into use by Locke.

The primary are extension, etc.; the secondary, smell, color, sound, etc. The "common percepts," given by him are the same as primary qualities given by Locke, Descartes, Reid, and Sir William Hamilton, viz.: Motion, rest, number, figure, magnitude.

Motion we obtain by touch and sight, and all the rest by motion.

He accounts for the apparent deception of the senses, by saying that not our senses, but our inferences from them deceive. He goes over the senses one by one to show this. The principal ideas given by sight are three; color, shape, and vision; sound, by hearing. Touch is the most important, as it gives us our knowledge of matter as matter.

Through the senses, he says, we get form, and not the matter; meaning that matter does not enter into mind. But Hamilton thinks he held the doctrine of mediate perception. This cannot be. Let us inquire for a moment into the term "common sense." By it we understand

good sound sense, an ordinary but still a very extraordinary thing, homely but very desirable. In the philosophy of Aristotle, common sense means the common percepts that are perceived by all senses. We have examined two faculties, the nutritive and the *αἴσθεσις*. There still remains a—

3d. The faculties of spontaneous memory, *μνῆσις*, and reminiscence, *ἀνάμνησις*. When will calls up something that does not now exist, we call it memory. The difference between spontaneous memory and reminiscence is this: spontaneous memory is such as we have in dreams; reminiscence is when the will begins to direct. Under this head he gives the analysis of the laws of association of ideas. These he reduced to three—similarity, contrast, contiguity.

We cannot call up a thing by a direct act of the will, except by these laws. Hobbs is the modern discoverer of these laws. Hamilton erroneously thinks that Aristotle hinted at our modern law of redintegration.

4th. Along with memory he places *φαντασία*. The objects presented by this is the *φάντασμα*, or image. Dogs barking in their sleep is an evidence of *φαντασία*. They see an image in their sleep. The word has been corrupted into fancy and phantom, which do not express the meaning. Philosophers are trying to convey it back to its original significance. *φαντασία* must be carefully distinguished from the power of forming conceptions.

5th. Above all these faculties he places the *νοῦς*, *mens*, or intellect. The *νοῦς* seems eternal. He divides it into—

Νοῦς ποιητικός, creative or active, and *Νοῦς παθητικός*, receptive or passive.

In regard to knowledge, man has a *δύναμις*. The boy and the infant have it. Suppose a boy have a natural taste for mathematics, that would be a *δύναμις*. The *δύναμις* can be developed; it takes the shape *ἐντελέχεια* when he has the readiness for knowing. When called forth it becomes an *ἐνέργεια*. He takes up another discussion, whether the intellect is the recipient of forms. He holds that it is. "The place of ideas and forms," he says, "is in the intellect." The intellect is the *τόπος εἰδῶν*, place of forms; but in capacity, *δύναμις*, and not in actuality, *ἐνέργεια*, nor in readiness for action, *ἐντελέχεια*. This capacity is innate.

Many capacities are never developed, but still are capable of development. Hence we shall stand up for original ideas. He was not a mere sensationalist.

The Logic of Aristotle.

Aristotle is the founder of Logic, although he was in a measure anticipated by Zeno, the Eleatic; just as the Copernican system was by Pythagoras. Logic, *τὸ λογικόν μέρος, τὰ λογικά*, was first used by the Stoics. Zeno founded dialectics; Socrates spoke of deduction and definition. In India there was a logic of five parts. Archytas' writings on Logic are forgeries. The logical treatises of Aristotle are six in number. These were never collected in one work; but together they constitute the "Organon." Strange to say, he has given us no definition of Logic.

The six treatises are:

Κατεγορίαι, divided into the ten heads or categories, which is a bold attempt to classify human knowledge.

Some have attempted to give us a new classification, or to modify the old, and Mill has tried to develop a new set.

The famous categories of Aristotle are:

Substance (*οὐσία*), Quantity (*πόσον*), Quality (*ποῖον*), Relation (*πρόστι*), Place (*ποῦ*), Time (*πότε*), Situation (*κεῖσθαι*), Possession (*ἔχειν*), Action (*ποιεῖν*), Suffering (*πάσχειν*).

The arrangement is objective, that is, what may fall under notice. Everything must come under one of these heads.

'Ερμηνεία treats of the interpretation of language as an instrument of thought. As instruments of thought, subject, predicate, copula, and inference are necessary. In the first part the elementary parts are treated; in the second, he treats of the compound parts; proportions, definitions, and judgments. He does not distinguish between conception, judgment and argument, but supplies such a distinction.

Αναλυτικὰ πρότερα. This and the next are the analytic books in which he treats of the syllogism. It is, according to his peculiar meaning, the analysis of the argument. It is, after all, the correct analysis of the mode of reasoning of the human mind. It cannot very well be improved, though Mill and Hamilton have attempted it. It does not profess to be a new mode of reasoning. Its plan is simply to bring together two terms by a third term, and to see if they agree or disagree.

'Αναλυτικὰ ὕστερα, in which he shows the application of conclusions, and what can be demonstrated from them.

Τοπικὰ διαλεκτικά. A speculative philosophy which he narrows to the logic of the probable. It is to be distinguished from another use of the word "dialectics."

Σοφιστικοὶ ἔλεγχοι, an exposition of fallacies. He distinguished between Formal and Material.

The Ethics of Aristotle.

Socrates was the founder of this science. He discussed it with great interest, and tried to show that virtue always leads to happiness, and that ignorance is wickedness.

Aristotle's books are as follows: Book I. An inquiry into the end, *τέλος*, at which all men aim. He said it was happiness, not pleasure, which he defines thus: "An energy of the soul according to the best virtue in a perfect life." It is difficult to understand. It means something permanent, eternal. It is more than a *δύναμις*, it is an *ἐνέργεια*. "Man is happy only so far as he energizes." It cannot be praised, for to praise requires a higher standard.

Books II. and III. Virtue. His definition is plausible, but not satisfactory.

Virtue, *ἀρετή*, not the same as the Roman virtue, which means bravery, nor quite so pure as our virtue. He defines it thus:

"It is a (1) habit, *ἕξις*, founded on and exercising deliberate preference in a mean relative to ourselves; (2) defined by right reason, and according to the definition of a man of moral wisdom."

Let us look at some of the words of this definition. The word for virtue is *ἀρετή*. This was an *ἕξις*, that is, a disposition of the mind and a choosing. It is not something natural, but acquired. Socrates represented it as consisting in wisdom. Aristotle says its seat is in the will. "All the virtues," he says, "are means between the two extremes." Thus liberality is a mean between extravagance and niggardly conduct; courage, between rashness and cowardice.

But it is determined by *λόγος* what it is. "It is defined by right reason." Notice, then, he brings in the will and the reason. Conscience he makes an exercise of the reason. In particular there is a union of will and understanding.

Book IV. A discussion about the will. It is not exhaustive. He distinguishes between three kinds: *βόυλησις*, *προαίρησις*, *βουλευτικόν*.

called organism not [illegible]
in himself
[illegible]
[illegible]
Sulphur [illegible]
Heads [illegible]
of things

[illegible]

CHAPTER III.

POST-ARISTOTELIAN SCHOOLS.

After Aristotle arose especially four sects called by Cicero disciplinæ, who professed to follow either Plato, Aristotle, or Socrates.

1. The Peripatetics, who regarded Aristotle as their founder. They are so called from his habit of walking about as they talked.

   By them his doctrines were carried to Arabia; thence to Europe, where, during the Middle Ages, his philosophy reigned supreme. It fell in the sixteenth century.

The commentators on Aristotle were:

Andronicus.

Alexander the Aphrodicean.

Philoponus and Simplicius.

We must know these in order to understand Aristotle completely.

II. Academy—professed to follow Plato: divided into three branches.

1. Old Academy; Xenocrates, Polemon.
2. Middle Academy; ~~Arcen~~taus, Cicero.
3. New Academy; Neo-Platonists of Alexandria.

Socrates and Plato taught two systems; the one searching, the other dogmatic. The former is taken up by Grote, the latter by Archer Butler.

Plato had two sides, the positive or ideal, and the negative or doubting. The latter was taken by the Academics. Speusippus was the first, and taught 347–339 B. C. He was followed by Xenocrates. These are of the "Old Academy." Next arose the "Middle Academy," the members of which did not follow

Plato so closely. Arcesilaus (315–241 B. C.) was the founder. Then came a later school, the "New Academicians," of whom Carneades (214–129 B. C.) is the founder, but Cicero, who attended the schools at Athens, and whose comments are the most valuable records we have, was the most illustrious member of the school.

III. Epicureans.

1. Epicurus (340–270 B. C.), of Samos, self-educated; professed to follow Democritus, but gives atoms free will. From love of philosophy he came to Athens 306 B. C. His philosophy was wide spread.
2. Lucretius—his greatest follower; great influence in Rome; one of the causes of decline of the Roman Empire.

Epicurean Philosophy:

a. Physics—Adopted Democritus' atoms; most refined were *media* of perception. Epicurus was not an atheist, but his school became so.

b. Psychology—Dwelt on the senses. He placed above them a πρόληψις. Above the names and by them, man has an anticipation which brings to the mind a motive εἴδωλον, of gods. Lucretius, however, was an atheist.

c. Ethics—Highest aim or final end is ἡδονή, pleasure. Virtue is the best means of reaching it, and vice of losing it. This was a popular philosophy; and adapted to the wants of men in general, It led to sensualism.

IV. Stoics.

When Paul went to Athens he found the Stoics and the Epicureans the two leading sects, both of which opposed him. Stoicism was a self-righteousness, making its followers, not only right before God, but equal with God. Epicureanism held up pleasure as an end. The founder was Zeno, of Ceturus in Cyprus, who, read-

[illegible]

[illegible]

[illegible]

[illegible]

[illegible]

[illegible]

[illegible]

[illegible]

[illegible]

[illegible]

[illegible]

[illegible]

ing Xenophon to drive away melancholy, was led to philosophy.

He went to Athens 320 B. C., and joined Crates, the Cynic, who taught that there was no other good but virtue. He lectured at the Στοά.

He was followed by Cleanthes, of Assos, in the Troas. He was Zeno's scholar. His abilities were slow, but profound. He has a hymn to Zeus, pantheistic but grand.

Next came Chrysippus, of Soli, in Silicia. He was a man of excessive acuteness. He bore the same relation to the Stoics that Zeno did to the Eleatics. He wrote five hundred lines a day, composing seven hundred and ~~five~~ works. The Philosophy pleased the stern Romans. Cato was the first Roman Stoic; then came—

Seneca, tutor of Nero, contemporary of Paul; a half Academician.

He was an elegant writer, almost as eloquent as Cicero. Seneca was the brother of Gallio, who "cared for none of these things." This may have been the common sentiment of the times. There were two other illustrious members of the school:—

Epictetus, (90 A. D.), an educated slave, who wrote a good book; and

M. Aurelius Antoninus, a Roman Emperor of the second century. He wrote ὑπομνήματα, τὰ εἰς ἑαυτόν, "Meditations upon himself." It contains the highest maxims of heathen morality. Pride is the only motive capable of reaching this high model.

The Philosophy of the Stoics. They first clearly announced the division of philosophy into—

1. Logic or Dialectics: the mode of enquiry.
2. Physics, which treats of things that are. It includes psychology and theology.
3. Ethics, which treats of things that ought to be. (This division of philosophy, though perfect, is practically useless.)

1. Logic. The Stoics were great logicians, especially Chrysippus.

N. B. Theophrastus, not Aristotle, introduced hypothetical reasoning.

The Stoics laid great stress on hypothetical and disjunctive reasoning. Categorical reasoning is only a modification of this.

Discussed also what was the origin and test of Truth: "*Nil est in intellectu quod non prius fuerit in sensu.*" Here they assumed that there is above the senses a disposing principle, ἡλεμονικόν. Plato's λογιστικόν, Aristotle's κοιναὶ ἔννοιαι—common sense). The Stoics were not sensationalists.

2. Physics, largely *a priori*. It assumed two *substrata*, agent and patient. The former equaled God, and was intimately connected with the other, matter. This latter cannot cohere without the active principle; neither can the latter inhere but in matter. Both are separable only in imagination. (Balbus Lactantius.) They taught that there are four elements, fire, air, water and earth.

The world is not infinite; the space beyond our sphere being assigned to fire, the heavy elements were unable to rise.

History of the World—

1. World is wrapped in fire.
2. Redeemed by moisture.
3. Fire consumed, rarified, purified the lower elements, filled the vacuum, and then receded.
4. Then came the atmosphere, and from it water. This sinking down, the land came forth. Finally vapors arose and æther was produced.
5. In water seeds were germinated, generating the world.
6. Infinite succession of conflagrations ('Εκπύρωσις) with intermediate cycles of repose.

This was an anticipation of the star-dust theory.

They taught that the gods are first formed, then the other objects of creation.

Nature of the Gods.

The Stoics identified the gods with fire, but that of a more etherial nature than what we perceive. They attributed to them moral, active, and intellectual powers. Plato, Saturn and Mercury were supposed to be renewed by fire. They believed in a πρόνοια, *providentia*, and a pre-ordained connection between things. This, they held, was revealed by augury. They distinguished between *Fatum* and *Necessitas*, holding the former, denying the latter. *Fatum* was spoken by God, and being the best possible, could never be changed. There is no defect in the world, because it could not be better; and no real evil, because all things are for good.

Immortality. The soul is separately immortal, till the ἐκπύρωσις, when it is merged in the fire, to issue at the next period.

3. Ethics.

Virtue is the highest and only good.

Virtue was to live according to nature: *i. e.*, there is a perfect plan in nature, and we are to fall in with it. M. Aurelius Antoninus says: "If anything else be supposed good, and anything but its opposite evil, we land in contradiction." Pleasure is not good, pain is not evil. Regulus was happy in the barrel of spikes. Seneca says: "Never seek pleasure, nor shun pain." They opposed the Peripatetics, because they thought pain to be an evil. Only the part of the body suffering is affected: the soul is calmed by the ἡγεμονικόν.

Τέλος, *finis*. They were struck with the beauty and harmony in nature, and with all things acting toward some end. They thought it the highest duty to co-operate in this grand harmony. Hence the expetible, "*per se*," is to live agreeably to nature. [Zeno, *Ζῆν ὁμολογουμένως τῇ φύσει.*] Thus they became keepers of Zeus.

In practice these doctrines brought themselves into difficulty. They resorted to distinctions, *παρά δοξα.*

Between Determinate, Positive, and Indifferent. *Διαφορά* and *ἀδιάφορα:* things either distinctly good or bad, or things to which no morality attached. These latter were:

α. *Προήγμενα*, to be chosen: such as life, health, strength, beauty, wealth, honor, nobility, etc.

β. *'Απροήγμενα*, to be rejected: such as death, sickness, etc., contraries to the former.

γ. Neither (*α*) nor (*β*;) all intermediate things are simply *ἀδιάφορα*, or indifferent.

Chrysippus connects all immediately with the intellect, which, he says, produces them. In every passion there is a notion; hence they are governed by intellect. He does not distinguish *φάντασμα*, and general notions. They form the idea of eradicating the passions by *ἀπάθεια*, because they are perturbations repugnant to our nature, *τα πάθη*, exorbitant appetites. N. B.—"They ought to be controlled, not done away with. But Stoics gave will no power over them."—McCosh.

(3). Suicide they thought right, but on other grounds than those of J. S. Mill. Their ground was incapacity for more pleasure: "When a man can no longer fulfill a good purpose, or lives without aim, he may consult the gods, *i. e.*, auguries, etc. If they favor his design, kill himself."—Cato.

Answer:

α. Man has no such right.

β. A man may seem to have no end to serve, and still have an end to serve, perhaps by the example of his suffering.

Pleasure and Good. These should not be placed upon a level, as in the Epicurean system of morals. Pleasure should never influence as a motive, though it may often follow as a consequence of virtue. Nor is pleasure a part of the highest good. The negative character of happiness consisted in peace of mind and freedom from disturbance.

Highest Good is Law. Our obligation to God, as a law, follows from our natural and rational character, as conformable to the arrangement of nature.

Emotions and Virtue.

Emotions are irrational impulses transgressing the right mean. Emotion is a movement of the ἡγεμονικόν, contrary to nature, and therefore wrong. They are called forth by the imagination, of which there are four faulty cases.

Idea of Virtue. Negatively, is defined as the being exempt from emotions; positively, a rightly ordered reason. It is an inseparable combination of will and knowledge; the former being indispensable to practical activity.

Conclusion and *resumé* of Ancient Philosophers:

A. The Peripatetics had but little influence.

B. Stoic philosophy held a very important place. It represented the high moral element, and as such it was adopted by the higher Romans. There was a very artificial system of morality, virtue being the only good.

C. The Epicurean philosophy had a mighty influence among the Romans. The higher Romans adopted Stoicism; the lower classes fostered Epicureanism, as the lower morals of such towns as Herculaneum were defended and endorsed by it.

D. Academics. Neo-Platonists in Alexandria took up the "highest points in Plato's doctrine;" but as to the other Schools, they were eclectic.

The Alexandrians adopted the positive side.

They took Plato's ideal theory, and said the highest exercise of mind is the ἔκστασις, the immediate beholding, the intuitive contemplation of the good. Such philosophers were:

(1.) Philo Judæus, in Paul's time. Used the word λόγος.

(2.) Plotinus, (205–270 A. D.) He wrote much, but is of obscure note.

(3.) Porphyrius, (233 A. D.) Author of the five logical divisions: genus, differentia, species, property, and accident.

(4.) Iamblichus, of the fourth century. Theosophy; wonder-workers.

(5.) Proclus, of the fifth century.

The first century was characterised by opposition between the Christian and heathen philosophy. After Justin Martyr many affinities arose between them. He was followed by Augustine and Origen.

At Athens, 522 A. D., by order of Justinian, the heathen schools were closed. Philosophy went to the Arabians. They brought it back to Europe. Christian philosophy introduced the idea of creation and holiness.

Close of Ancient Heathen Philosophy.

Alexandria was at this time one of the most populous cities of the world. It was full of all nations. About the time of Christ there were 300,000 Greeks, 300,000 Jews and others, within its walls. There, too, was the famous Alexandrian library and museum. Then the East and the West met and fomented, and a school arose which tried to choose the best traits of the philosophy of the East and that of Greece. It was called the Eclectic School and became the Neo-Platonic, which took the ideal side of Plato, the side of positive truth.

They said that the mind, by a contemplation of the good and true, could rise to a higher state, called ecstacy, that is an immediate gaze upon the one and the good. They set themselves against Christianity by setting up something higher. They said that it brought down the pure and good to the level of our low nature. The views of the Bible, they said, were anthropomorphic.

Heathen philosophy expired in the emptiness of Neo-Platonism. This was one of the last forms which Grecian philosophy assumed. It was an eclectic spirit drawing from East and West, from India and Persia, and the analytic philosophy of Greece. It allied itself with miracles, and became a system of imposition. It had no influence upon the great mass of men; and even among its votaries it spent itself in mere abstraction.

Christians hold that the contemplation of the good God is the highest exercise which the mind can reach. This school closed 522 A. D., at command of the Emperor Justinian. It had existed since 600 B. C.

Rise of Christian Philosophy.

It rose among the disciples of Christ in the second century.

Transition period—

(1.) The Christian idea. The turning of self-consciousness upon itself forms the starting point of the new philosophy. The self-consciousness had not yet become sufficiently absorbed in itself to look upon the true, the Divine, in any other light than as separate from itself and belonging to all opposite world.

Neo-Platonism tried to overcome this separation, but all in vain. Christianity took up the problem. It assumed for its principle that the human and Divine could be united in one. The speculative, fundamental idea of Christianity is, that God has become incarnate; and thus it unites the two.

(2.) Scholasticism. Christianity naturally came in contact with the contemporaneous philosophy, especially with Platonism. In the ninth century an attempt was made to continue Neo-Platonism with Christianity, though it was not till after the eleventh century that there was developed anything that might be properly termed a Christian philosophy. This was the so-called Scholasticism. Its great effort was to reconcile religion and the reflecting self-consciousness, or faith and knowledge.

Such was the transition period of the Christian philosophy. The first example of the Christian philosophy is—

a. Justin, the martyr. He was born 103 A. D., in Palestine, and died a martyr, 167. He wrote an apology on the Christian religion while retaining certain elements of Platonism. He was a Platonist before he became a Christian, but he was not allied with Epicureanism or Scepticism. But somehow, Christianity was often thus allied with Platonism, to its injury. Epicureanism and Stoicism did not associate so much with Christianity. Men admitted philosophy, and a false one, into their religion. This charge cannot, however, be made against Justin.

Origen. He was born at Alexandria 183, and died 253 A. D. He was a man of great genius, strong mind and good character. For many years he was at the head of the Alexandrian School. He was noted for his great speculative capacity. His great work was "First Principles." There are some very profound speculations in this, and some truths. He sought to combine Christianity with Neo-Platonism and the Eleatic philosophy. He desired something grander than the latter. He unfolded a system of development and identified Jesus with the highest development. To him Bishop Butler owes the suggestions for his great argument.

Tertullian. He was born at Carthage. He was at first extremely hostile to Christianity. He was deeply impressed by the courage of the martyrs. After his conversion he wrote a work of very great power, called the "Apology of Christians."

Augustine, (356–430 A. D.,) was the most profound thinker and influential theologian of the early church. His influence was confined mostly to the West. He was the wayward son of a pious, praying mother. By profession he was a rhetorician, and followed the philosophy of Aristotle. In the meantime he was given over to vice. All along, however, he was convinced that he was in the wrong and against God. At length he became a Christian. As a speculative thinker he was equal to Kant, Locke, Aristotle, or Descartes. His psychology was ahead of his times and entitled him to a rank with Aristotle and Leibnitz. Lastly, all great theologians examine his writings to see what were his views on various topics. Thus we find, in the border country between philosophy and religion, certain great thinkers; and we find men all going back to Aristotle through them. Augustine introduced all the important views of the Middle Ages. The Schoolmen took their views of Aristotle from him. (We call them Schoolmen, not Fathers, after the ninth century.) He had more influence over the thought of the Middle Ages than Aristotle, though, to some extent, he got this by applying Aristotle's views. So the doctrines of the latter were accepted through him. According to Hamilton, he originated the doctrine of the association of ideas, and defined beauty as

the result of harmony and design. He originated the argument for the existence of God. He reduced all laws of association to the one law of beauty.

We have now the introduction of a new philosophical element:—the idea of God and his attributes; the relation of knowledge to faith; the nature of God and of the infinite. The idea of God as holy and infinite was as new as it was grand.

PERIOD II.—THE MEDLÆVAL OR SCHOLASTIC PHILOSOPHY.

It is represented as beginning about the sixth century and lasted one thousand years. It was brought about by the decay of the Roman Empire and extended to the light which broke in upon the sixteenth century. It began when the barbarians broke in upon the haunts of civilization, breaking up those institutions which were fettering freedom of thought. True it is that the people were subject for a time to more barbarous laws; but the desire for knowledge excited among the barbarians by their subjects, soon led to the planting of schools. They began to be established in the seventh century in common with monasteries. In France, during Charlemagne's reign, ten or eleven of them were founded. At that time Europe was very ignorant. Alfred the Great tells us that in his time but very few priests could understand the formulas in their readings, much less write their names. In this state of things the church introduced monasteries and universities. The course of study at one of these was twofold:

1. A *trivium*, embracing grammar, dialectics and rhetoric.
2. A *Quadrivium*, embracing geometry, arithmetic, music and astrology.

These were called the seven liberal arts. Their dialectics included logic, and was represented as a woman of awful countenance, holding a serpent in one hand and a hook in the other.

At Oxford the student received a smattering of grammar, then the dialectics and categories and rhetoric followed. Few ever studied geometry. Music was subservient to the church service. Astrology was filled with mysticism and speculation.

But even this formal introduction attracted many. Oxford had three thousand scholars in the year 1200, and afterwards had thirty thousand during the reign of Henry III.; and during that time there were ten thousand at Bologna, and twenty-five thousand at Paris. At the present time, as far as respects Oxford, there are not half as many. It is clear, then, there was a great thirst for learning, though there was not much to be learned.

The philosophy of the Middle Ages consists of two things: logic, and the application of logic to theology.

We shall speak especially of the latter. They did apply logic somewhat to physical science, and sought to construct a system of physics. Their philosophy, however, consisted chiefly in the application of logic to theology. No one looked, then, for physics. It is to be remarked that their knowledge of Scriptures was second-hand, for their knowledge of Hebrew was small, and but few could read in the original. They studied by translation. They applied logic to this translation, placing the subjects of the Bible, as well as all other things, under some of Aristotle's categories. They tried to put them under heads, and some of their divisions are yet in use. They kept up spirited discussions; and it is to them we owe many distinctions found in all modern theology, distinctions found in every branch, which Mill says cannot be set aside. But now let us turn more especially to the logical discussions. There were several who were engaged in these.

John Scotus Erigena (800–877). He wrote a work called "*De Divisione Naturæ.*" His great ideas were of oriental origin. His writings are by some attributed to Dionysius the Areopagite. He was Irish, and not Scotch. With him God is all, and nothing but God is real. He thus lands himself in Eastern pantheism. He is not truly a schoolman; that philosophy dates from the opening of the next century. Porphyry says, "I wish to speak of genus and species, whether they subsist in the nature of things, or are mere conceptions; whether corporeal or incorporeal." Boethius says, "They are real existences."

Roscellinus was a native of France, who lived in the eleventh century. He decided the question started by Porphyry in a different way from Boethius. He wrote a work on "Faith in the Trinity." He is represented (we hear accounts of his doctrine from his opponents only) as maintaining that genera and species have no real existence, are only words. But said his opponents, "How do you account for the Trinity? for this makes the persons in the Godhead mere names." He said there were three different gods. He was persecuted for his opinions and had to flee from his country. St. Anselm opposed his erroneous doctrines and refuted them. Roscellinus was a Nominalist. Aristotle was not a Nominalist.

Anselm (1033–1109) was a Realist. He came from Aosta, in a valley of the Alps, and studied in Normandy. He entered the order of St. Benedict, and afterwards became Archbishop of Canterbury. It is to him we owe a famous argument, *a priori*, that has been discussed by Descartes and others, for the existence of a God. It is taken from the text, "The fool hath said in his heart, there is no God." If the fool says so, he shows that he has a conception of God, forms an idea of divinity. Whatever is conceived is in the intelligence; but a conception, than which no greater can be had, implies a corresponding reality. Man has an idea of a perfect being; hence, this idea has a reality, that is, God exists. It has been replied that man can conceive of an island in the middle of the ocean, but that does not argue the existence of the island. Anselm, however, does not argue from the mere conception, but from the peculiar nature of the conception, "than which no greater can be conceived." The original is found in Augustine. Confusion arises from the "than which no greater can be conceived." Whatever man conceives, he thinks there may be a greater. We think that the universality of the conception is sufficient proof.

Abelard (1079–1142), a native of France, born near Nantes, opposed both Realism and Nominalism. He was educated at Paris, being a pupil of Roscellinus. No one has yet been able to determine what his opinions really were. His distinctive doctrines are:

a. He is now spoken of as the founder of Conceptualism, which says that general notions consist not in real things, but in conceptions of the mind. Cousin says he makes one fight with the other. To the nominalist he opposes this principle, that nothing exists but individuals and particulars. To the realist he shows there is no real substance but the individual. He maintains that universals cannot be only words, for they must be something, while words are nothing. But " universals are neither words or things," says Cousin, " they must be only conceptions of individuals."

b. The relations of faith and reason. Anselm said, "*Crede ut intelligas.*" Abelard said, "*Intellige ut credas.*" The relations of faith and reason is one of the great controversies of the day. Hamilton maintains that the basis of all knowledge is faith. Mansel, in " Bampton Lectures," uphold's Anselm's view.

c. Theory of abstraction. " The individuals have resemblances which the mind can perceive, and an abstraction being made of their differences, classes can be formed. This is distinctly Conceptualism."

Abelard was said to be the greatest of the Schoolmen. When he taught in Paris, he had three thousand students, and when he returned to the country they followed him and dwelt in tents.

He enjoyed a wonderful popularity, but led a troubled life, because he became obnoxious to some of the leading ecclesiastics of his time, especially St. Bernard. He was opposed by—

Peter Lombard. He was born in Lombardy, studied in Paris. He died 1160. He was called " Magister Sententiarum." His work, four books of *Sentential*, was a collection of the opinions of the Fathers upon principal points. It was long used as a classical text-book. It was the characteristic of an age that was bent down.

John of Salisbury (1110–1180) was born in England. He studied in France. He tells us logic was the reigning science in his time. He has given us the fullest description of Nominalism and Realism, but complains that the youth spent too much time in idle controversies upon elementary rules and forms. He wrote often in poetry. His works are in four or eight volumes.

Albert of Cologne (1193–1280) was called Albertus Magnus. He wrote on Universals and Conditionals, and endeavored to introduce Aristotle's doctrine, combining them with the reasoning of the Schoolmen. His pupil was—

Thomas Aquinas (1228–1276), the "Angelical Doctor," adhered to the doctrine of Augustine. He wrote *Summa Logica*, in which he taught to embrace all doctrine, divine and human. He exalted the understanding as the highest principle. He wrote a treatise on morals and logical subjects, besides commentaries on all the philosophy of Aristotle. His writings are very elaborate. His defect is that he endeavored to do too much. He is the highest authority of the Church of Rome, and was a man of great ability.

John Duns Scotus, the Doctor Subtilis of the schools, was a Franciscan and differed from Thomas Aquinas, who was a Dominican, on the basis of free will and predestination. The Franciscan monks opposed predestination. He exalted the will as the highest principle. Both were Realists, but Scotus held that the universal existed *formaliter*, while Aquinas that it existed *realiter*. His pupil was—

William of Occam, who is represented as the reviver of Nominalism. He is called Venerabilis Inceptor. Dean Mansel says he was a Conceptualist. His logic is very valuable; the most valuable of the Middle Ages, says Mansel.

In the 15th century philosophy began to decline. This was due (1) to the growing taste for physical science under Roger Bacon, Galileo, Francis Bacon and others; (2) to the rise of Greek learning. Greek books were spread over Europe at the downfall of Constantinople; and (3) to the universal spread of the philosophy of Aristotle.

A Realist is now rare. We have one—a Mr. Morris. Nominalists are numerous, as Whately, Hobbes, Hume and Stewart, Mill. There are also many Conceptualists, as Locke, Reid, Kant, Hamilton and Brown.

There is a truth in Realism; for if individual things are real, common attributes are also real. Without generalization and naming, the work would be lost; thus there is a truth in Nominalism. But it is the conception of objects possessing common qualities which is the universal, which makes a class one. When this is present, all is present; when wanting, all is wanting. Realism errs by excess when it says the universal can exist separate from the individual. Nominalism errs, not in common terms, but by overlooking common properties. Conceptualism is the true theory when not misrepresented. It was because Locke tried to find some mental image that he failed. Mill, who is not favorable to the Schoolmen, says that the the distinctions they drew were perfect. We are daily using them.

Discussion is now between Conceptualists and Nominalists.

Mediæval Philosophy.

A Review of its Developments.

It began in the 6th century, was confined chiefly to monasteries and universities. The philosophy of these Schoolmen consisted in the study of pure logic, and in the application of logic to theology.

A. Logic having been investigated by Aristotle, was put in its present form by them. They discussed, among other things, Realism, Nominalism and Conceptualism. There is a truth in each.

1. In Realism. *Universalia ante rem.*

(1) The mind has a tendency to resist general conceptions.

(2) The individuals die, while the typical forms exist independently

(3) Moral law always reigns. It is prominent.

Their error was in ascribing to universals an existence independent of the singulars. This, however, was the orthodox doctrine of the church. It resembles the idealism of Plato, the objective reality of the universals. Plato maintains the existence of the idea in the divine mind.

2. In Nominalism. *Universalia post rem.* (Aristotle.)

Words certainly aid the mind in abstract reasoning. But is forgotten by those holding this doctrine, that these must be of objects in the mind, in order to get a general term in the apprehension of a class. It is forgotten that classes exist in nature. This is the revolutionary doctrine, and bears the same relation to Realism as Aristotle to Plato.

[illegible] κοιναι
ἐπιστολαι [illegible].
[illegible] in
ch. of Rome - [illegible]
Protestant - only [illegible]
[illegible] Constantine's [illegible]
[illegible]
[illegible]
Councils - not [illegible], but [illegible]
unity [illegible]
founded by [illegible]

3. In Conceptualism. *Universalia in re.*

This is the true theory, but it takes a wrong form when it regards the conception as an idea or image, from which we form the class. It also errs if it overlooks the utility or necessity of signs. If it avoids these errors it is true; for in general notions, the essential thing is to group objects by common properties. We get from things themselves, that by which we are able to classify them. This is the intermediate opinion.

B. The second feature of the mediæval philosophy was the application of logic to theology. Under this we find many profound subjects discussed. St. Augustine reigned in theology as Aristotle did in logic. He was the authority on all points of doctrine. The principal feature of this discussion lies in Anselm's argument for the existence of God.

By discussing the relations between Reason and Faith and the reality in universals, the schoolmen (*a*) preserved the seeds of knowledge, through those long middle ages, and (*b*) they kept alive a spirit of thinking, and thus those who followed them had their faculties sharpened to a wonderful degree. Their scholarship was high.

A good picture of these times is found in "Romola."

PERIOD III.—MODERN PHILOSOPHY.

CHAPTER I.

TRANSITION TO THE MODERN PHILOSOPHY.

The emancipation of Modern Philosophy from the bondage of Scholasticism, was a gradual process. Just as soon as the fundamental premise on which the Scholastic theology and method rested, *i. e.*, the rationality of the dogma, was abandoned, the whole structure fell to inevitable ruin. Yet, notwithstanding, Scholasticism was not without its positively good results. It had grown out of a scientific impulse, hence naturally awakened a free spirit of inquiry and a sense of knowledge. It made the object of faith the object of thought, and thus opened a sphere of doubt and investigation.

The revival of classics contributed positively and prominently to that change in the spirit of the age which marks the beginning of the new epoch of philosophy. The study of the ancients had almost entirely ceased in the course of the Middle Ages. But now the study of the classics in the original was revived. Thought took a different form. Sometimes a Platonist arose, professing the lofty theories of that great writer, wearied of the study of the Aristotelian logic. In Germany, also, classic studies found a fruitful soil. Melancthon was impressed with the Scholastic philosophy. Reuchlin and Erasmus labored in the classic movement; and though it was hostile to the Scholastic impulse, still it favored most decidedly the growing tendencies to the Reformation.

To all the above causes and symptoms of the intellectual revolution of this period should be added the starting up of the natural sciences and the inductive method of examining nature.

Roger Bacon (1214–1256) is said by some to have anticipated Francis Bacon. While he anticipated Francis in the study of physical science, he did not lay down or propound any system. He may have known, as did Aristotle, that the mind began with particulars and proceeded to generals. But he did not furnish a system out of this, nor did he show that he understood the inductive method. He was always discontented with the Scholastic spirit. He was superior to Francis, in that he actually turned to physical investigation and saw the importance of science better than Francis. But he gave no laws for its prosecution.

Francis Bacon now gave a great impulse to the study of nature. Galileo had begun before his time. Francis was the son of Nicholas Bacon, who held the great seal of England during the reign of Elizabeth. • He was born in London, 1561. At the age of thirteen he entered Trinity College, Cambridge. He and Newton have given it its reputation. At the age of sixteen he left with a profound contempt for the studies pursued there. He traveled on the continent for a time and then devoted himself to the study of the law. He was made Lord High Chancellor of England and Keeper of the King's Seal under James I. Being too ambitious of fame, he was subsequently expelled from these offices. He died in 1626, with a character which has not been without reproach. Pope says of him, "he was the greatest, the meanest and the wisest of mankind."

In 1605 he published his first treatise, "*De Augmentis Scientarum*;" in 1620 his "*Novum Organum*." Then he sought to combine all in his "*Instauratio Magna*."

In his first work he discourses on the hindrances to learning, the advancement of learning, the places and books of learning.

Errors and Obstacles to Science.

He arranged these under four heads, calling them εἴδωλα. What he meant we cannot exactly tell. Some think he used the word in the Greek sense, "false appearance;" others prefer the Latin, "objects of false worship."

1. Idols of the Tribe, (*Idola Tribus*). These are those common to all mankind. They spring from human nature.

They are of two kinds:

a. When one is under an influence greater than the love of truth.

b. When, being under the influence of truth, one is hurried on to careless and hasty generalizations, *e. g.*, the propensity to generalize history. "The mind is like a mirror, not a plane mirror that reflects objects just as they are, but one of uneven surface, which combines its own figure with that of the object which it represents." It is applied as against the tendency in men to build up more on the superstructure than the foundation will bear, *e. g.*, the attempt made to explain all mental phenomena from the laws and facts of electricity. The materialistic and atomic theories and the modern doctrine of development are further examples of this. There are many other absurd conclusions drawn in the present century, some of which claim to be founded on the principles of Verulam.

2. Idols of the Den (*Idola Specus*). They arise from the peculiar character of the individual as to his country, age, religion, profession, personal character, etc. "Each man," says Bacon, "has his own den, which refracts and impairs or obstructs the light of nature, in the dimness of which stands a divine idol." Some minds observe differences; others likenesses. The farmer maintains that there is nothing like farming. The merchant thinks he is all-important. Books tell us there is nothing so desirable as literature. There are some things peculiar to lawyers, to soldiers; and certain things are prejudicial to students.

3. Idols of the Market Place (*Idola Fori*). There are errors resulting from universal habit in the use of terms, which we have either not distinctly agreed upon, or which we do not clearly understand. We are often misled by language. They arise from the intercourse of society, "prejudice of the company." Men believe that their thoughts govern their words, but by a certain reaction their words govern their thoughts. Locke and D. Stewart treat of this error. Condillac refers all evils to language; but there may be evils of thought, as well as of language.

4. Idols of the Theatre (*Idola Theatri*). Those which rise from the dogmas of famous actors and false systems of philosophy. In the opinion of Bacon these are like so

1) A [illegible] makes [illegible] [illegible] [illegible] [illegible] [illegible] [illegible] [illegible] [illegible] [illegible] [illegible] [illegible] [illegible] [illegible].

2 The [illegible] ideal [illegible] truth.

By study [illegible] [illegible], [illegible] [illegible] [illegible] + [illegible]

3.

Then [illegible] [illegible] [illegible] [illegible] [illegible] [illegible] [illegible] [illegible] [illegible] [illegible] [illegible]

many forms or shows, dressed up like comedians, and brought upon the stage of the world. He had a special reference to Aristotle. Little did he think, when he wrote it, that his system would be perverted, as Aristotle's was, and he be accused for his "*Idola Theatri.*" Yet it was even so. There are persons now who give undue place to Bacon.

5. And now, in this age of speculation, we feel like adding another set of idols, *Idola Desertorum*, "Idols of the Wilderness." These arise from too great a spirit of independence. Men striving to fathom the unknown fall from the direct way, and depart from the truth.

In the *De ~~Argumentis~~* Bacon expounds the province of science, and gives a classification of the sciences.

A. *As to the Sciences.*—He divides them according to the faculties of the mind. He has three faculties—

1. Memory.

History
- Secular or Civil.
- Natural.
  - Regular Phenomena.
  - Monstrosities.
  - Arts.

2. Phantasy.

a. Fine Arts.

b. Poetry.
- Narrative.
- Dramatic.
- Parabolic.

3. Reason.

a. Divine Philosophy. Our knowledge of God, founded on Revelation, is not knowledge, but faith. Natural Theology, although sufficient to refute Atheism, is incompetent to establish religion. "We ought not to submit the mysteries of God to human science or reason, but to raise the things of reason to God."

b. Human Philosophy.

a. Physics. Contemplating what is inherent in matter and transitory, discovering two of Aristotle's causes, material and efficient.

β. Metaphysics; by which, through final causes, we rise to the contemplation of God. Two causes are here discovered, formal and final.

B. *As to knowledge.*—The test of the value of science is by its fruits. It is good in itself, but if it bring not forth good fruit it is not a genuine science, *e. g.*, Light is a good thing, but we value it for what it shows us.

Method.

In the *Organum* Bacon expounds his method, which some metaphysicians credit to Aristotle. But while Aristotle was in truth following the method, yet his was no anticipation of Bacon. Bacon said there were two modes of reasoning in use, and both were defective. The "*Novum Organum*" set aside the methods formerly employed, the empirical and the rational.

The empirical began with the investigation of facts, but only a few facts; and then rises immediately to general laws, rearing a pyramid on its point.

The rational method proceeded from pure thoughts to the nature and laws of things, and to the construction of a system of the universe. Now, Bacon undermines both of these and takes up the method of "induction." There are means employed, but only after a long course of induction and careful observation of facts. He condemns the Schoolmen because they deal with words and not realities. He was prejudiced, also, against Aristotle, against whom a reaction was then in progress. This reaction continued three hundred years, even down to our day.

His system is especially developed in his logic. The key-note is found in the opening clause: "Man is the minister of nature, not the master." Man is not to set himself above it. He says: "We must proceed by observation and collection of facts." These must be properly noticed and registered. Here he is seeking a condensation of facts. You must observe even those things and facts which seem opposite to laws. You must not set aside any, [illegible] [illegible] [illegible]

[illegible] [illegible] [illegible]

[illegible] must be [illegible]

[illegible] [illegible] [illegible] [illegible]

[illegible] [illegible] [illegible] [illegible]

[illegible] [illegible] [illegible]

[illegible] [illegible] [illegible]

[illegible] [illegible]

but collect all. Out of these facts gather first of all minor axioms. These axioms, as we call them, are not those so called by Euclid. But then he does not mean first truths. Euclid means common concepts of common opinions. Bacon meant the same as we mean by law *i. e.*, generalization. We must seek these minor axioms, and then not go on too rapidly. Both determination and precision are necessary. Then we rise to middle axioms; these are useful in the common affairs of life, being general statements; then to major axioms; finally, to "forms" and "causes." By forms he probably means the properties of things, which make them what they are. Thus by the form of heat he means that which makes heat what it is. He speaks of motion as the form of heat. He used Aristotle's four causes. He had an imperfect knowledge of how they could be applied to mind.

Bacon had two maxims:

1. "In proceeding you must make necessary rejections and exclusions." He means by that, to take phenomena and generalize; you must then make distinctions. This would be now called "analysis," or, as Dr. Whewell says, "decomposition of facts."

2. "You must co-ordinate facts, and beware of anticipating nature." He suggested a *tabula rasa* of mental phenomena. His plan was promoted as much by his genius as by his precepts. In his view of the mind he did not clearly see self-consciousness.

Review and Conclusion of Francis Bacon.

His great work, "*Instauratio Magna*" is not complete. It was to be composed of four parts. He is the author of what is called the new method. I believe it is a branch of logic, and not a metaphysical or physical science in a large sense. We owe that method to Bacon; not to say that it was not thought of before; Aristotle did think of it; every one that thinks or reasons does. By the process of induction men discovered the state of the weather. We owe to it the discovery of the heavenly bodies. Aristotle used it in his natural history. What I claim for Bacon is:

1. He first made it a subject of reflex investigation.
2. He first gave an explicit and decided account of it.

3. He first set men out on a systematic pursuit. Almost better than his method was the spirit he brought over science. His method has stood the test of the excellencies of a system. As it is shown in religion that faith should be made known by works, so in philosophy faith should be made known by works. Bacon has been misunderstood. He has been represeted as saying that science is to be appreciated only as practical, and valued only for its fruits. He takes his analogy from religion. His system cannot be fully understood by any one not acquainted with the doctrines of religion. He likens science to faith. Faith is to be tested by its works, not valued by them. So Bacon says faith is to be tested, not valued, by its works or fruits. He holds we must make some decomposition of facts. We must not leap at once to highest ground, to highest generalizations. He said we may rise also to final causes. What was the precise teaching of Bacon on final causes? Aristotle and Bacon agree. Bacon uses the causes given. He allots to metaphysics formal and final causes. He despised those who mixed up final and efficient causes. In the very age in which Bacon lived, Harvey argued for the circulation of the blood, from the existence of final causes.

(Best edition of Bacon by Speeding.)

He was not so great in life as in ability.

Macauley makes three charges against him:

1. Of courting the nobility.

2. Of betraying his friendship for the Earl of Essex. Bacon warned Essex, and sought to stop him in his mad career. It has been proved that his estate, supposed to have been given him, was in compensation for his services as a lawyer, or his own by hereditary right.

3. Of taking bribes. In answer, it is urged—

1st. That others did so at that time, and it was not then thought criminal.

2d. That most of them were given to his servants, as perquisites, which Bacon never got himself. But he confessed his fault with deep humiliation and contrition. In short, he is not as great morally as intellectually.

Tabulated estimate of Bacon as a philosopher.

A. Excellencies—

1. His method is the true one, used in all science.

2. We owe it exclusively to him. Aristotle began with particulars which were examples. The experiments of Roger Bacon and Galileo did not develop the theory, though employing the method of induction.
3. He gave a stimulus to the study of nature.
4. Kept inquirers from error, who mixed speculation with induction.
5. Had an enlarged spirit and comprehensive mind.
6. Had a good mode of exposition, style witty, full of fancy and imagination.
7. It is wrong to say—
    a. That he was a sensationalist. (Started by Locke.)
    b. That he discarded final causes, for he gave it place in metaphysics.
    c. That he valued science exclusively by its practical fruits: science is good in itself, but if it brings no good fruit, it is no science.
    d. He sets highest value on "forms." The highest aim of all science is to discover them.

B. Qualifications.

1. Men observed and practiced induction before him, *e. g.*, Archimedes, Galileo, and the Babylonian astronomers.
2. Improvements in the exposition have been made by Stewart Mill and Hume.
3. Wrong in thinking that inventions may be made by mere art or industry.
4. Unjust toward the Aristotelian method.
5. View of final causes defective.
6. Classification of science imperfect.
    a. The faculties in many places blended.
    b. His list of them very imperfect. He mingled the sciences and the arts.
7. Imperfect views of conducting mental sciences. Descartes remedied this.

CHAPTER II.

RENÉ DESCARTES.

René Descartes was born March 31st, 1596, at La Haye, in Touraine. At an early age he entered a Jesuit College at La Flèche, passed through philosophy, and graduated with little favor. Like Bacon he found little satisfaction in his studies, except to find out his own ignorance. He was a volunteer in the Imperial army, serving under Maurice of Orange and Tilly. Descartes was twenty-three years old when he began to investigate truth for himself, in his solitary quarters on the Danube. He laid down four rules for his guidance. He was a great mathematician, author of the idea that geometry treated of the relation of quantity. He first expressed geometrical curves by algebra; hence, formed Algebraical Geometry. At thirty-three he retired to Holland, and there courted retirement, not having found sufficient mental freedom in Paris, whither he had gone after leaving the army. But he was persecuted by the divines of the Utrecht University. Bœthius charged him with pantheism. Christiana invited him to her capital, whither he went. He returned to Paris, and died in 1650, at Stockholm. The period of Descartes' philosophy was, therefore, the first half of the 17th century. He was the first to give an explanation of the rainbow. As a mathematician he stood by the side of Newton. He was skilled in physics, whose phenomena he explained by the theory of vortices. He invented the geometrical and analytical methods in mathematics. But he acquired his great fame as a philosopher, the "Father of Modern Metaphysics." His principal works are—

1. "Method of Conducting the Sciences." "Set aside all prejudice and prejudices." "Believe naught unless you have sufficient evidence." (1637.)

[illegible] blessing

Math only [illegible] of quantity,

[illegible] [illegible] & Stadium.

[illegible] as may be [illegible] found [illegible]

by [illegible] good [illegible]

[illegible] [illegible]

[illegible] [illegible]

[illegible] This is [illegible]
[illegible] too

[illegible]
[illegible]

2. "Meditations on First Philosophy." (1641.)

This came from Aristotle. He, like Bacon, uses the Aristotelian phrases. We would call it metaphysics. It was an investigation into causes for the right conduct of life.

3. "*Principia Philosophiæ.*"

4. "His Responses."

These were made to the criticisms of Gassendi, of France, Hobbes and others. They are very brief and pointed; and to them we must look for a thorough knowledge of his philosophy, and the exact distinctions of his system

He has been charged with drawing from Bacon; but it is not so, for he quotes Bacon only once, and that in an unimportant discussion.

Philosophy of Descartes.

His method of rightly conducting reason in the sciences, some supposed to be an induction applied to the human mind; this is an entire mistake.

The Cartesian is the joint "dogmatic and deductive method.

He makes an assumption in that he is dogmatic; so that he may have something to start from.

He adduces certain other truths from this assumption. This is deduction.

In short, he was a great mathematician. Mathematics are founded on assumptions, as in Euclid. We do not think this to be the right method in philosophy. He felt himself not entitled to assume anything till he had tested or examined it. He must not only doubt what others believed in and said, but also what he himself believed in must be doubted. Hence the Cartesian doubt. This was not scepticism, but a simple doubt of all till proved, a simple state of hesitation. Doubting is thinking, therefore he laid down his fundamental assumption,

"*Cogito*, or *Dubito, ergo sum.*" From this he deduces his entire system. It is objected by eminent men that it is unfortunately expressed, for in the *ergo* there is an inference, a reasoning. Hobbes, Gassendi and others reduce it to a syllogistic form. Whatever thinks is; I think, therefore I am. The assumption is found in the supposed major premise. Cousin defends it, making *cogito* a mere primitive judgment. Emanuel Kant has a profound and powerful criticism on it. Are we to regard it as a process of reasoning? If it is so, it is either *petitio principii*, or its conclusiveness may be doubted. If the "*cogito*" be understood as embracing the "*ego*," that is, be understood "*ego cogito*," then the *ego* is evidently involved in it; is in fact assumed, and the proof is a paralogism. If it means anything short of this, then it might be difficult to establish the accuracy of the inference. Thus if the "*cogito*" does not embrace the "*ego*," it is not clear that the conclusion follows. He should have assumed neither alone. Or, are we to regard the statement as a sort of primitive judgment, as Cousin says, not implying mediate reasoning or a middle term? Taken in this sense, it would seem that the connection between thought and existence is involved in our knowledge of self as existing, rather than that the knowledge of self issues from the perception of the connection between thought and personal existence. Or are we to look on the expression as simply a mode of stating an assumption? In this case the word *ergo*—the usual symbol of inference—comes in awkwardly; besides, the truth to be assumed is not the complex judment, "*cogito, ergo sum*," but the fact revealed to consciousness of "*ego cogitans*," "I catch myself thinking." Now from this idea of self he gets something without himself. This idea is of such a kind that just as in the very idea of a triangle it is implied that all the angles must be equal to two right angles, so this idea of myself is of such a kind as that there is implied the existence of something without.

Argument for Divine Existence.

He finds within himself this idea. He assumes that the mind has an idea of something else. It is the same argument as Anselm's, but in a different form. He finds in himself the idea of the perfect, and argues that in this idea the existence of something infinite and perfect is implied, and there must be something to correspond to this;

hence a God. Or in other words, he argues that in this the idea of a God is comprised, as the equality of the three angles of a triangle to two right angles is comprised in the idea of a triangle. This is the great *a priori* argument. He has another argument for the Divine existence in what he assumes as a fact, that God has implanted an idea of the infinite in our minds.

This is *a posteriori*. He has now derived—

1. His own existence.
2. The existence of a perfect being.

Mind and Matter.

He now finds within himself two ideas—

1. The idea of space or matter.
2. The idea of mind—Leibnitz adds potency.

The essence of the former is extension, of the latter thought, feelings. Thought here is meant to stand for all emotional phenomena. These preliminaries are essentially distinct in the mind, and all human ideas belong to the one or the other. Therefore he concluded that the substances whose fundamental attributes are respectively thought and extension, are themselves necessary distinct. Matter fills all space. There is no such thing as a vacuum. In his brief "Responses," (Descartes was not a voluminous writer) he gives an argument for and against the possibility of a vacuum. It is argued by some against him that there must be motion. Descartes says space is like a circle: one body occupies the space before another goes out. He rejected indivisible elements.

He has, then, two ideas in the mind. But now he asks does matter really exist? The idea of the perfect does imply the subjective existence of a perfect being, but the idea of the existence of matter does not imply or argue that, there is matter. How reach it, then? The idea of extension and of the existence of matter is in all minds. I could not make it. It was from God who made mind. God who is perfect implanted it there, and would not have permitted such an idea to arise in the mind were there no corresponding object. How would he deceive us? It would be a contradiction to suppose it. Hence he finds his argument for the existence of matter in the Divine veracity.

Malebranche, the Christian Plato, did not admit the consequences which Descartes inferred. "The idea of a body," he said, "did not involve the existence of a body." Being a Roman Catholic, he held the doctrine of transubstantiation, which saved him from Idealism. Berkeley, "the great Irish metaphysician," felt himself attracted to the doctrines of Malebranche, whose monastery he visited while traveling in France. The latter is said to have died from the irritation caused by the discussion.

We cannot prove that there is matter. We perceive it intuitively, immediately. But this did not suit this mathematical man. He makes a single assumption and builds all over it, and thus assumes too little. Reid, in the next century, did better, and said we must assume the existence of matter, as well as the existence of mind. It is substantially said by Hamilton that we know matter immediately; and that it is for men to assume, not merely "*cogito*," but to inquire what are the things immediately known. The great inquiry now is, what can we legitimately assume? As, for example, some think that parallel lines can never be proved but must be assumed.

Seat of the Soul.

Descartes supposed the soul to be situated in the pineal gland in the centre of the brain. Since the other parts of the brain are double, if the soul were in any of them, all perceptions would be double. These views are unsupported by proof, although Huxley sets value upon this.

Innate Ideas.

He says that they are not found in the minds of children and savages, but that they had a capacity for them. The two tests are clearness and distinctness.

Descartes was driven to consider the lower animals as higher forms of automata. Prof. Huxley endorses him, either in jest or earnest.

Attributes and Modes of God.

Descartes drew the distinction between attributes and modes of God, maintaining that everything which exists is

a mode of God; hence, his conception of God includes sin and like ideas.

Substance.

Descartes and Spinoza differ from Locke in not making substance a support, but that which exists in itself. Descartes, however, admitted two substances, mind and matter; Spinoza, most consistently, only one.

Estimates of Descartes as a Philosopher.

A. Excellencies—

1. Spirit of independence. He submitted every opinion to a sifting examination.
2. His method was the dogmatical deductive, of which he is a fine example.
3. He drew the distinction between mind and matter more clearly than ever done before.
4. He taught us to look within.
5. Correct in his assumption of innate ideas.
6. He was right in giving idea of an infinite and perfect being a prominent place. Aristotle in his Physics mentions two aspects of the infinite, that which is beyond our widest conception, and that to which nothing can be added.

Defects.

1. In Method (*a*) incorrect for mental science. It is appropriate for mathematics, but not for a science of scattered facts. (*b*) He assumed too few principles. He built a pyramid on a point: He assumed mind, but not matter. Reid claimed both. This is the superiority of the Scotch school.
2. His tests for innate ideas are unsatisfactory. We can clearly and distinctly conceive error.
3. His way of arriving at matter is circuitous and wrong. "Veracity" is not conclusive.
4. He reared the theistic argument on too narrow a basis. He based it on the idea of the perfect. To complete it it is necessary to bring in the teleological argument.

5. His view of body is defective; body has energy as well as extension.
6. He separated mind and body so far that they could not interact. He made men and brutes mere machines.

The Cartesian School.

The most illustrious of this school was Malebranche; not so clear a writer as Descartes, but an able philosopher. His philosophy had two peculiarities:

I. Occasional causes. This resulted from his accepting Descartes' distinctions between mind and body. It is this. Man is not a true cause but an occasion. When I will to move my arm, my mind cannot move the arm, but God moves it.

Objections to this are (*a*) when murderer will his deed, God performs it. (*b*) It differs from our ideas of causation, *i. e.*, same cause produce same effect.

Malebranche drew a distinction between sentiment and idea. Sentiment is human and personal; idea, like Plato's, divine and impersonal. He distinguished between primary and secondary qualities of matter.

II. Vision of all things in God. We see extension, space, etc., in God.

Port Royal Logic is the best work of this school; in it the distinction between the extension and the intension of a motion was first drawn.

CHAPTER III.

BENEDICT SPINOZA.

Benedict Spinoza was born at Amsterdam in 1632. He died in 1677, at the age of forty-four. A Jew by birth and education, he was taught in his boyhood to read the Old Testament and Talmud. In his youth he exchanged these pursuits for the study of physics and of Descartes, yet he was dissatisfied with the consistency of the Cartesian system, especially with the consistency of the logic. He thought it should go further; this led him into pantheism. He soon came to an open rupture with the Jews who excommunicated him. He then left Amsterdam and settled near Leyden. He finally went to the Hague, where he spent his life in the greatest seclusion, devoted wholly to pursuits of study. He never married. He supported himself by grinding opera-glasses, which his friends sold for him. He was invited to a professorship at Heidelberg, with full permission to teach as he chose; but he declined, because it would involve him in controversy.

He proposed to proceed on the doctrine of Descartes. Descartes had defined substance as that which needs nothing else in order to its support. Spinoza modified it. "By substance," said he, "I mean that which is in itself conceived by itself, *i. e.*, that of which the concept can be formed without having need of the concept of any other thing." In other words, that which is self-comprised and is conceived by and through itself alone. He started with this, and comes to the conclusion that there is only one substance, of which all other things are only the attributes or modes. He argues in a mathematical way with a great array of distinctions and word-quibbling. He built his whole philosophical system upon this idea of substance.

His definition of substance. "*Per substantiam intelligo id quod in se est et per se concipitur, hoc est, id cujus conceptus non indiget conceptu alterius rei a quo formari debeat.*" There is a whole aggregate of things jumbled in this definition. That which is in itself is one thing; that which is concerned by itself is another thing. He says, "if there be two substances they must be either like or unlike. If altogether like, they must be one and the same thing; and if unlike, how could they produce each other, for like produces like." To meet him the disciples of Descartes drew many distinctions. They did not mean to say that substance was independent of God; as to its cause, it might need a Divine being to create it. Thus the predominant idea of Descartes was cause; of Spinoza, substance. Spinoza clothes substance with extension and thought. Descartes had two substances, body and mind. "But," said Spinoza, "we cannot have two substances, for like produces like." What he finds in man, he also finds in God. God is the highest extensive concept. He makes him to have perceptions essential to his nature, and always present; eternity, goodness, infinity. Thus, through Spinoza, we get our introduction to modern speculative pantheism. It did exist, no doubt, before, but he was the real founder of it, and the first to develop it. It is difficult to get hold of, for it assumes various forms. But with Spinoza, it is both physical and spiritual. He draws a distinction between attributes and modes of extension; attributes are what are essential to things; modes are mere adventitious exhibitions of the attributes. The objects in this world are hence modes of the Divine Being.

He introduces the doctrine that there is life in everything. It rises as we go from matter to animals, and is highest in man.

His Ethics.

He begins with definitions and then gets axioms, proceeding in the "joint dogmatic and deductive method," thus drawing a number of propositions. These axioms are not always legitimate, and his definitions often very faulty. This led him to many monstrosities, from which

all shrink. His doctrine banished all idea of accountability and all fear of a judgment day, and broke down the foundation of all morality; and yet he was a man intoxicated with the idea of a God.

Let us sum up his peculiarities.

1. He was a great system builder, proceeding on the joint dogmatic and deductive method, setting out from assumptions, definitions and axioms.

2. He professes to follow Descartes, but it is doubtful whether he argues from the Cartesian view of substance. They draw a distinction, and say that they did not mean to say that substance had no need of God to support it, as a cause of it; but being created, it did not require any other substance to uphold it.

3. His definitions are arbitrary; his axioms not self-evident. He endeavors to show that things could not produce each other, unless alike. We see this contradicted in the polar forces, where like produces unlike. Why should not God, then, produce a universe different from himself? But causation does not exist in likeness, but in power. We are not sure that things altogether like are the same. Every one thing has an individuality of its own. He was met in this way. Take two drops of water exactly alike, are they the same? No; they are numerically different, if they differ in no other way.

4. He overlooked principles as clear and certain as those he proceeded on, *e.g.*—

(1.) We know self as differing from non-self.

(2.) We know our own personality; *i. e.*, we are persons.

(3.) We carry along with us a sense of responsibility arising from conscience, which gives us a sense of law to which we are accountable to a being different and higher than ourselves.

These truths have no place in Spinoza. But we must always carry these with us. They are the principles which undermine pantheism.

5. He constituted a hideous system. He did not shrink from any consequences to which his system led him, *i. e.*, God stole, killed, committed adultery, when man did.

(1.) He recognized no distinction between the Creator and the creature. To meet him we must examine his assumptions, which being overturned his whole system falls.

(2.) He made no distinction between good and evil. Sin, adultery, cruelty are all modifications of God, and are sanctified by Him. He modified the Old Testament to suit his own views, adopting all those passages in which God is represented as being present in all his works. "In him we live and move and have our being."

In Great Britain we find a number of eminent men in the first half of the seventeenth century; such as—

Lord Herbert of Cherbury (1581–1648). He was a deistical writer, an original but not a clear thinker, certainly not a graceful writer. He was a man of great learning and rare dignity of personal character. He wrote a treatise, "*De Veritate*," an elaborate pleading in favor of deism. He also endeavored to show the analogy of things. He says there are innate ideas in the mind, some of which he derives from religion. His five common notions of natural religion are: (1.) That there is a God; (2.) That he ought to be worshipped; (3.) That virtue and piety are the chief elements of worship; (4.) That repentence is a duty; (5.) That there is a future life, with rewards and punishments.

Then we have a body of English divines who mainly discussed the question between Aristotle and Plato, not yet as between Locke and Descartes, concerning the nature of ideas. They held that the idea was something in the mind and born with it. In this there is much truth, but also much confusion; deeper than sense and experience.

Then there were the Cambridge Platonists, all of whom maintained that there was something in the soul prior to sense, but requiring sense to call it forth. This they were fond of describing as connate or connatural.

Henry More wrote an apology, called "*Conjectura Cabalistica.*" He held intellectual intuition as the source of all philosophical knowledge; and maintained that all true and legitimate notions, which philosophy possesses, proceeded from Divine revelation. Reality, he said, consisted in extension, &c.

Ralph Cudworth, (1617–1688), the author of "The Intellectual System of the Universe," which was translated into German. He maintained innate ideas in the sense of

Plato, and derived therefrom a proof of the Divine existence. He distinguished between occasion and cause. He also defends the doctrine of "immutable morality," discovered by reason.

Among the Puritans were—

Richard Baxter, who appeals to first principles of morality. [*Vidè* Intuitions, *p.* 86.]

John Howe, chaplain to Cromwell, wrote various theological books, among which was his "Living Temple." In this he shows the state of thought at that time. Locke was regarded as a reformer, when he opposed those divines.

Cudworth stands up for an immutable morality discovered by reason, and, like More, distinguishes between occasion and cause. The Puritans, generally, applied the first principles, intellectual and moral. Thus Baxter says: "And if I could not answer a sceptic who denied the certainty of my judgment by sensation and reflexive intuition, yet nature would not suffer me to doubt. By my actions I know that I am, and that I am a sentient, intelligent, thinking, ruling and operative being.

CHAPTER IV.

JOHN LOCKE.

John Locke (1632–1704). He was the oldest son of a father who always exacted the greatest respect from his sons. He was educated at Westminster School and Christ Church, Oxford. We are still shown the mulberry tree he planted, and beneath which he loved to sit. He did not approve of the course at Oxford, and was sorry he ever went there. Writing to Lord Peterborough, he would have him omit nothing that would develop the mind. He never had a profession, but applied himself to the study of the physical sciences, and especially of medicine. Dugald Stewart says it was the best preparation for his mind. He undoubtedly saw the necessity of applying to the study of metaphysics the inductive method of Bacon. In 1664 he accompanied Sir Walter Vane, as his secretary, on a diplomatic mission to Brandenburg. He described his experience with a good deal of humor, as his letters show. Returning to Oxford in 1666, he refused a flattering offer, made him by the Duke of Armond, of considerable preferment in the Irish Church. He thought himself not able to fill the place, and declined on the ground that he did not experience that "internal vocation," without which no one ought to enter the priestly profession. In 1666 he became acquainted with Lord Ashley, afterward the Earl of Shaftesbury. This acquaintance brought him into intimate relations with Halifax, Sheffield, and others. In 1670 he sketched, for a number of his friends, the first plan of his famous Essay on the Human Understanding. The completed work appeared in 1689. In 1672 he was nominated and elected Secretary of Presentations, which office he lost at the first fall of his patron. In 1675 he visited France for his health, and his journals and letters are not only valuable for the accounts, though unfavorable, they give of the

French society at that time, but also are exceedingly amusing, animated and gay. In 1683 Locke went to Holland, where he found a safe and tranquil retreat during the evil days of tyranny and persecution. In 1685 he left Amsterdam. At this time he wrote his famous letter on "Toleration." In 1687 he first printed it in Latin. The Revolution of 1688 was the triumph of those free principles of which Locke had been the proclaimer and martyr; and he now returned to England in the same fleet which conveyed Queen Mary from Holland. He was now appointed a member of the Council of Trade. On his return to England, he became acquainted with Newton and others employed in the public service.

He had several good treatises on different subjects. After short service Locke retired from public employment, and for some years took up his residence with an accomplished and intellectual woman, Lady Masham. He died October 28th, 1704. When about to die, he said that he had spent a happy life.

His Personal Appearance and Character.

Prominence of bones and features, an expression showing decision. His very look shows he cannot be dishonest. He thinks for self. His personal character seems to have been one of those which approach perfection as nearly as can be expected from our fallible and imperfect nature. He lays down rules for the guidance of the thinking powers. But he did not attach so high a place to the feelings and moral power. He was a little too self-dependent. If he had learned to distrust his judgment more, he would have done better. Still we always feel we are in a pure atmosphere when we are with him.

His Style.

Good manners are the blossom of good sense. The loss of kindness in the heart leads to ~~ill~~ manners. His style was rather that of a man educated in and by the world; not that of a student, but plain and conversational.

Essay on Human Understanding.

In this he shows all his powers of close deduction and accurate observation. His object was to give a rational and clear account of the nature of the human mind; of the real character of the idea and the mode in which it is presented to the consciousness. (See Shaw's Manual of Eng. Lit., p. 249, *et seq.*)

Analysis of the Essay.—There are four books, viz.:

1. Showing that there are no innate ideas, neither speculative nor practical.

2. Showing how our ideas do spring from the materials that come from sensation and reflection.

3. Treating of the nature and properties of language; of its relation to the ideas of which it is a vehicle; and of its abuses and imperfections.

4. Treating of knowledge, its degrees, extent and reality.

A Summary of his Philosophy.

He begins by showing that there are no innate ideas, then leads us to the definition of ideas. He says, "Idea is that which stands for whatever is the object of understanding when the mind thinks. I have used it to express what we mean by "phantasm—notion or species."

Book I.—A Negative Treatise.

(1.) There are no innate speculative ideas or principles. He takes an example from the Scholastic principle of contradiction. "It is impossible for the same to be and not to be at the same time." The infant has no such principle before the mind, and the savage cannot understand it. Therefore the child and the savage have no innate ideas.

In his position regarding innate ideas, he opposed Lord Herbert, of Cherbury, who held that they existed.

(2.) There are no innate practical principles. There is no common consent as to moral truth. He cites the views of other nations: at Sparta, deceit was encouraged; in India, infanticide. But perversions of these practical principles do not prove their non-existence, any more than difference of opinion proves absence of intellect.

[illegible]

(3.) He takes up certain ideas supposed to be innate, and shows that men do not agree on them; *e. g.*, he shows that some men have no ~~conception of~~ the idea of God.

But there may be innate rules or principles, even if not innate ideas. There are connate ideas and fundamental laws of human belief. He shows that no positive ideas are objects of understanding.

Locke is right when he says there are not innate abstract idea or general maxims in the mind before consciousness; but there are innate principles there, working as aptitudes or tendencies which enable us to distinguish the true and the good. These generalized maxims are discovered by induction.

Book II.—Positive.

He here shows how we get all our ideas from Sensation and Reflection. "External and internal sensations are the only passages which I can find," said he, "to the understanding." "They are the only windows which let light into the dark room. Would that the pictures would stay there and be orderly!" He makes two inlets, then, of the soul. There is an old maxim, "*Nihil est in intellectu, quod non prius fuerit in sensu*," which Locke has been charged with maintaining. But this is a mistake. He has two inlets; the one internal, the other external. By them we receive all our materials for ideas. He set out to show that. Locke's Sensation=αἴσθησις=Reid's "perception" =Modern "sense-perception." His Reflection=our Self-consciousness, without power of self-cognizance.

We have ideas from sensation and from reflection. He made sensation equal to sense-perception. Reid afterwards distinguished between them. This shows that Locke was not a Sensationalist.

The ideas obtained from Sensation are primary, those from Reflection are secondary. Hence comes the great distinction between primary and secondary qualities of matter. The primary are extension, Solidity, Figure, Motion, Rest, Number, Situation, Texture. From these come all our ideas of body. The secondary qualities are such as color, sound. Primary are found in body, in whatever state it is. Secondary are not. Reflection gives us all we know of mental and spiritual states.

From materials thus furnished, our faculties work out ideas. These faculties were:

1. Perception; that which perceives the idea; equals simple *apprehension*. It seems at times as if he made the idea and perception different, although he insists that they are the same.

2. Retention; meaning the same as memory; retains ideas.

3. Discernment; distinguishes between ideas.

4. Comparison; by which we perceive resemblances.

5. Composition; which puts old things in new shapes.

6. Abstraction; which separates a part from the whole.

7. Volition; by which we will to do a thing.

Now, by all these we form out of the materials furnished all that is possible. His first ideas are either simple or complex.

1. Simple, in the sense of original. These we get from sensation and reflection. They give us:

a. Space, given by two senses, sight and touch.

b. Time, solely derived from reflection, *i. e.*, reflecting upon ideas passing in the mind. Consciousness has to do only with what is in the mind. Memory must come in to give idea of time.

2. Complex, because they are fashioned by the mind by joining the simple. These are his three categories:

a. Substance. Here he gets into difficulties. His views are obscure. He does not deny substance, but says the mind is necessitated to believe in something underlying qualities, that is, *substantial* substance. Stillingfleet charged him with undermining the doctrine of the Trinity.

b. Modes, such as triangles, gravitation, etc.

c. Relations. These are well classified: whole and part, cause and effect, etc. He speaks, also of adequate and inadequate ideas.

Ideas of power and infinity. In contemplating things without us, we find one producing the other. The idea of power comes from sensation and reflection. Outside, we see the blow; inside, we know we move the arm by volition. Hume says, "that power, being derived from the

senses, is merely antecedents and consequents." He thus undermines the true theory of cause and effect.

The idea of infinity is derived from sensation and reflection. The infinite is a purely negative idea. It is that which has no bounds. His language is inconsistent and vague. He touches upon the association of ideas, but does not expand.

Book III.

In his third book he treats of the relation of ideas to language. He follows out Bacon's view that many errors come in from language. In fact he is so absurd as to say that it is doubtful whether we get from language more good than evil. D. Stewart carries out and exaggerates this view. Cousin justly criticises them, showing that the error lies not in the language but in the confusion of ideas, which causes the confusion of language. He inquires as to what is the meaning of abstract and general ideas, and he fails to distinguish between them. The Schoolmen did this very perfectly. Nevertheless, he distinguishes between phantasm and general notion. He is in fact a conceptualist. By idea he means simply an image. He inquires into language. He laid down many important maxims relating to error.

Book IV.

In the fourth book he gives his definition of knowledge. The true definition is the correspondence of ideas with other things. But he defined it: "The perception of the agreement or disagreement of our ideas with one another." Locke was a Realist, but he could not be so consistently. His definition of knowledge as the correspondence of ideas, not to objects, but to each other, lands him in Idealism. We can never perceive ideas of themselves. These come in from without, and we cannot prove they correspond.

In the same book he treats of intuition. He says that intuition is the immediate perception of the agreement or disagreement of our ideas. Intuition, with him, consists merely in the comparison of ideas. He treats also of reason, and confounds it with reasoning. Then he examines the philosophy of Aristotle, and shows himself not well acquainted with it. He treats of reason and faith like Abelard. He magnifies reason, but says that faith often transcends reason. He said: "We believe many things not contrary to, but above reason." He was a sincere believer in the word of God. Locke's views of the syllogism were defective. He seemed to consider it a peculiar kind of reasoning, whereas it is really only the unfolding *explicitcr* what is contained *implicitcr* in all reasoning. H was met on this point by Archbishop Whately.

Locke's Excellencies.

1. His spirit of independence; his candor and love of truth.
2. We see that he is following professedly the right method. It is that of observation. He was the founder of modern psychology, as Aristotle was of the ancient.
3. He set aside forever certain views of innate ideas, such as Descartes and Lord Herbert held:
   a. In the sense of *images.*
   b. In the sense of *abstract notions*, or general notions.
   c. In the sense of *principles* before the mind as principles.
4. He has given a most admirable account of the way in which, by abstraction, the mind gets its ideas from materials. This is given in the second book, which on this account is very valuable.
5. His most useful remarks are on the relation of words to ideas; *vide* Book III.
6. His particular expositions were often better than his system as a whole, *e. g.*, his intuition and demonstration.
7. He has important remarks on every metaphysical subject.

We have seen that just previous to Locke's appearance all philosophers thought it necessary to protest against the authority of Aristotle and the Schoolmen. Bacon and Descartes were very much dissatisfied with the instruction given in the colleges, because of its unfruitfulness and sta-

[illegible]

[illegible] Bild [illegible]

[illegible]

[illegible]

tionary character. The continual disputes about modes and forms, universals, identity, etc., had wearied the mind, and there was a realistic reaction. Grotius and Puffendorf, in Holland, had recommended the study of nature as more profitable. The latter applied himself to law and jurisprudence. There seemed, also, a desire to apply to the investigation of the human mind the experimental method, which has been so very successful in physical science. This was the question when Locke, in an upper chamber, was attempting to solve a knotty problem for some friends. He concluded it would be best to examine our own abilities before we attempted to solve such subjects.

The Deficiencies of Locke.

1. He might have arrived at more truth had he suspected himself a little more. He was a little too self-sufficient, too confident in his own powers.

2. He begins with too resolute an intention to derive all our ideas from sensation and reflection. He begins with his theory and tries to establish it by facts—a faulty method of procedure. Mill has defended him, but unsuccessfully.

3. He commenced with the discussion as to the origin of ideas, before considering the ideas themselves.

4. He overlooked those native principles of the mind, such as that of cause and effect, which underlie the exercise of the faculties. There is something which constrains the mind to seek the cause after the effect.

5. He did not see that these principles themselves furnished ideas.

Perhaps we may here, as well as anywhere, speak of the origin of our ideas. The old Stoic maxim is that all our ideas come from the senses. Some people have charged Locke with endeavoring to maintain the same; but he expressly names the two inlets, sensation and reflection. Now, thinking, moral approbation, etc., you cannot get from the senses; and Locke was too keen a man not to see this. "No," says he, "we get them from reflection." Can we get them from either of these two? No. He was met by

Leibnitz, a very able man, who takes up his essay, chapter after chapter, and criticises it. "Time," says Locke, "we get by reflection on the succession of our ideas." But without time, how can you know there is succession.

6. It follows that his attempts to explain time, power, the infinite, and moral good, leave out the peculiarity of the idea; *e.g.*, the explanation of moral good leaves out the obligation, ought. He did not meet the rising scepticism.

7. In the use of the word "idea" he confounds the phantasm, which comes from the reproductive faculties, and notion, which comes from the comparative faculties. The distinction had been made by the schools, but he confounds these throughout his essay.

8. He supposes the mind looks rather at ideas than at things. His definition of knowledge is "agreement or disagreement of our ideas with one another." This brings us away from realities, and lands his doctrine in Idealism, though he was far from professing to be an Idealist.

9. His view of knowledge is very defective. He calls it agreement between ideas, whereas the mind begins with things.

10. His views of the necessary principles of mind as axioms, maxims, etc., are especially defective.

11. His account of the ideas and nature of moral good is very defective. Moral good he gets from the idea of pleasure and pain, with a moral law superadded. But where this law?

Locke's Essay was vigorously opposed on its first appearance. He was met in his own day by Stillingfleet, Bishop of Worcester; but was not vanquished. Stillingfleet maintained that Locke's account of substance was not deep enough, and that he opposed the doctrine of the Trinity and of the immortality of the soul. It was said that he had not laid sufficient foundation for virtue and morality. Moore and Cudworth maintained that there were deeper foundations than Locke's.

Locke's Contemporaries.

Dr. Samuel Clarke, a man of vast erudition, of great logical power, and discursive ability. He was a friend of

Sir Isaac Newton, and developed his philosophy. He proceeded in a mathematical manner, like Descartes.

1. He demonstrates the existence of a God and His attributes.

2. He gives virtue a place among mental perceptions, and defends free-will and responsibility. His view of virtue is that it "consists in the fitness of things, or a congruity of relations." He neglects the distinction and prior discernment of good ends from bad. This view has been condemned by the Butlerian School and modern moralists as being too limited and confined.

In 1704 he delivered the Boyle lectures, in which he brought forward his celebrated argument *a priori* for the being of God: grand in conception, but, like all arguments of that class, resting on the *a posteriori* element, expressed or implied, for he assumes as a fact that man has an idea of space and time. This he says is a necessary idea; and when we come to inquire into the nature of space and time, they must be either substance or modes. They are modes of a substance, and that substance is God. His is a rational view of morals. He and Newton represented time and space as qualities (which is a mistake) and then represented reason as a guaranty that these qualities implied a substance in which they adhere, *i. e.*, God. Clarke argues powerfully that space and time are realities, but makes them attributes, properties or modes of an eternal substance, God.

Butler (1692–1752) was the greatest ethical writer in those days. He treats of appetites and affections. Affections are Benevolent, altruistic, and Personal, egoistic. Above all these he places Conscience, which he treats of more fully than any other writer before him. He makes it supreme over all voluntary states of the mind.

Excellencies.

1. He classified motive powers as appetites, affections and conscience.

2. He showed that man is not a purely selfish creature.

3. He demonstrated the supremacy of conscience.

DEFECTS.

Are negative rather than positive.

1. He does not see that the decision of conscience does not make an action good or evil, but that as the eye it simply perceives the quality of the act.

2. He does not state that virtue implies an act of the will.

3. He does not distinctly show that conscience condemns.

CHAPTER V.

BERKELEY AND HUTCHESON.

George Berkeley was the Bishop of Cloyne, in Ireland, his native country. Born in 1684, and died in 1752. He was educated at Trinity College, Dublin, and acknowledged to be a man of great ability. Like Plato's, his system is put in the mouths of interlocutors, and thrown into the form of dialogue. His grand object was to defend religion, both natural and revealed, from the materialistic tendencies of the times. It is doubtful whether he did it much service, however, for it can be defended on other grounds. He was a great mathematician, and was continually reasoning upon the subject. He tried to prove to mathematicians that there could be no such thing as infinity, and argued about the minus quantity. He became a high favorite with all parties. He was beloved by Swift, Steele, Addison and Pope. Bent on philanthropic projects, he conceived a plan of Christianizing the American Indians, by establishing a college in the Bermudas. After living two years in Newport, R. I., he gave up his design, and returned to England. While in America he wrote the "Minute Philosopher." His most important contribution was his new "Theory of Vision," which was published about 1709, and in which he showed successfully that the eye is the percipient of nothing but colors; and again, that the mind is not directly cognizant of distance. This latter perception is not intuitive. This he was enabled to gather from the famous Cheselden and Franz cases. [See '79's Notes on Psychology, p. 28.]

His Principles of Philosophy.

I. 1. Theory of Vision, [*vide supra*]. 1709.

2. Idea. His idea is an image which has its exist-

ence in God. There can be no idea of abstractions. He is not a Nominalist nor a Realist, but an Individualist.

3. In every state we know ourselves as existing.

II. That the existence of substance cannot be proved; that this idea serves the purpose of a support. He denies substance to matter and gives it to mind.

III. Matter. The common idea of his theory is that he denied the existence of matter. But this is a great mistake; in fact, he expressly states that he does believe in matter, just as you or I do, and believes in it thoroughly. Says he, "That which I see, hear and feel doth exist—that is to say, is pèrceived by me. I no more doubt it than I do of my own being." But he differs as to what is matter, and adds: "I do not see how the testimony of the particular sense can be alleged as a proof of the particular existence of anything which is not perceived by sense. Now, you say there is a substratum which I do not see; but here we differ. I do not believe in the existence of a 'substratum.' I say it has an existence as an idea. That of unthinking things without their *esse* is *percepi* (*esse est percepi*), nor is it possible they should have any existence out of the minds of thinking things that percéive them. When we do our utmost to conceive the existence of external bodies, we are all the while contemplating our own ideas." Some one put the question about things in a desert, where no one could see them; and he answered, they were before the contemplation of God. He says, "I believe matter exists, but not the same matter." He strove to undermine the Materialist. "You make," says he, "matter to explain mind, but you must have mind to perceive matter." Many, even of the present day, are going back to him and cling to his theory. Many followers of Sir Wm. Hamilton, and especially his successor, Mr. Frazer, incline to his doctrine.

Estimate of Berkeley as a Philosopher.

A—Excellencies.

1. He was a man of great purity of character. He was a poetic genius, though his poetry was written in prose. He was a man who set a high aim and steadily pursued it.

[illegible]

[illegible]

III [illegible]

[illegible]

2. He established the fact that, intuitively, we do not know objects at a distance. There had been anticipations of these views. They were confirmed by the Cheselden case. Berkeley held that to the infant, intuitively, a solid mass will appear a surface.

3. He showed that the mind could not bear an adequate idea of a general notion in the sense of a phantasm. He landed himself in Nominalism.

4. He drove to its logical consequence Locke's doctrine that the mind is originally the percipient of ideas only.

5. He was right in saying that there is no substance in the sense of a substratum or support. Locke maintained that there was something invisible underneath, which kept the properties in their place and supported them. But there is no reason to support this substratum; no proof of it in the consciousness or senses. Neither is there anything in the reason that requires a belief in it. Substance is that which has being, permanence and potency. This is sufficient; and Berkeley did good by putting it on this basis, and removing the substratum. [*Vide Princeton Review, January*, 1873.]

B—Defects.

1. His theory was a failure, for it did not meet the rising scepticism and materialism of the day. He wished to, but failed.

2. The mind may have an intellectual notion which is higher than a phantasm. We can conceive of things as possessing common properties; *e. g.*, rose. We cannot think of the same rose as being red and white at the same time, but we can abstract the quality redness from it, and apply it to a class of roses. This he did not see.

3. It is quite true that we are not to suppose that there is anything in the object but what we cognize. But, in opposition to this, we do know the object itself, and we know it as a substance, that is, as having being, permanence and potency.

SCOTTISH PHILOSOPHY.

There is a unity in its method and spirit. It has three points which distinguish it.

1. It proceeds on the method of observation, professedly and really. Ancient speculations did not proceed on the method of induction; no doubt they had some facts, but the phenomena served only as a starting point with them. They proceeded on a dogmatic-deductive method. But this spirit was banished by Bacon and Newton, and the establishment of the Royal Society in London. Bacon said his method was applicable to all sciences, both of mind and matter. By it one could arrange a history and tables of anger, fear, etc., just as well as we can form tables of natural things. Their employment of the inductive method was slow. Some say Descartes proceeded on it, but it was not so; for, although he made use of facts, it was only as a starting point, and not to develop laws. Hobbes did not pretend to go on this method. Locke proceeds very largely in observation, but he nowhere professes to follow induction. He tries to establish from facts a preconceived theory. We claim, then, that the Scottish school have the honor of first following the inductive method, systematically and throughout. The schools in France profess to do it, but only as "Empiricists." Reid and Stewart announced that the mind was to be studied.

2. The Scotch Philosophy employs self-consciousness as the instrument of observation. Bacon had no clear idea or apprehension of the instrument to be used. In respect to means of observation, we are greatly indebted to Descartes. He taught men to proceed on the great internal deas. Locke also appeals to the internal sense. But the iScottish school took a step beyond all the rest; they are thus distinguished from those who try to explain mental action by physiology. There is nothing, however, in the school to disparage the close inspection of the body in connection with the mind. But physiology was too little advanced at that time, and not in a state calculated to give much philosophical knowledge. The Scottish school strenuously maintained that it was not by mere chemical analysis but by inward feeling that we know our mental operations. Introspection, however, is irksome and difficult, when thought is rapid or feeling intense. We must take a survey of the thoughts of others, and from their actions, conversations, and the looking on the steady flow of our

a

2

own ideas, discover our mental operations. Reid thus often refers to the action of other men.

3. By the observation of consciousness principles are reached which are prior to and independent of experience. This is a great characteristic of the school, distinguishing it from empiricism and dogmatic-deductive method and *a priori* observations. It maintains that we can discover principles independent of experience. These are somewhat differently described by different men of the school. Reid designates them as common sense: Stewart as "fundamental laws of thought and belief;" Hutcheson calls them "moral sense;" Brown, "principles of induction;" Hamilton, "*a priori* forms or conditions."

The above-mentioned school has thrown much light upon the mind, the association of ideas and the classification of mental phenomena, throwing aside error and establishing fundamental truth. The transcendental Germans have gone to extreme. The Scotch is the philosophy of consciousness. We do not maintain that they discovered all truth or all discoverable truth. Sir William Hamilton discusses many great subjects, yet to many they are unsatisfactory. Reid and Stewart thought to establish philosophy after many years of patient labor and research. Brown and Hamilton departed from this method and established systems.

Merits.

1. Valuable contributions to English literature.
2. It has done much to keep the world from error.
3. Classification of the faculties is of great value.

Francis Hutcheson (1694–1746). He was the founder of the school. His father was a Scotchman, who emigrated to the northeast of Ireland, where Francis was born. His father's name was Alexander Hutcheson. Francis was educated at Glasgow. He followed Shaftesbury. He published many works, dwelling on his (Shaftesbury's) works, especially on the moral sense. Locke had two, one an external, the other an internal sense. Shaftesbury introduced others.

He dwells on the native and moral parts of man's nature more than any other. He especially discussed "Sense of Beauty" and "Sense of Virtue." By this moral sense we have our original ideas.

His definition of sense: "Every determination of our minds to receive ideas is independent of our will." [*Vide* Ueberweg, Vol. II., p. 392.]

HIS CLASSES OF SENSES.

1. External Senses, universally known.

2. Pleasant Perceptions, arising from regular uniform objects, *e. g.*, pleasant imaginations.

3. Public Sense, our determination to be pleased with the happiness of others. This inward passion cannot be a sense.

4. Moral Sense, by which we perceive virtue or vice in ourselves or others; *e. g.*, benevolence.

5. Sense of Honor; a sense of approbation, ideas of decency and dignity.

He says this enumeration is not sufficient. There are other senses in certain circumstances. We have now five senses. Locke gave us two inlets to the soul.

He next shows how secondary grow upon original desires. These secondary must arise from the original in proportion to the strength of the latter. The secondary imply the primary. James Mackintosh says he seems to be the first to give the secondary senses.

He shows also how we get association of ideas. He does not stand up for beauty in the nature of things, independent of the perception.

Excellencies.

1st. Founder of Scottish School, although Hamilton gives the honor to Gershom Carmichael.

2d. Spread a taste for elegant literature and philosophy over Ireland and Scotland.

3d. Opposed the selfish theory of humanity.

4th. Brought in Moral Sense.

5th. Element of truth in all his writings.

Defects.

1st. Moral Sense not happy phrase. It is an inlet of knowledge, but not like bodily sense.

2d. Virtue consisted in benevolence, thus leaving out justice. Edwards improved this by making it love.

3d. His Ethical system is derived too much from heathen or pagan philosophy.

CHAPTER VI.

DAVID HUME.

David Hume (1711–1776) was born at Edinburgh, a place rendered romantic by Scott. He was the second son of Joseph Hume, a lawyer. There are two accounts of his life; one by himself, the other by Mr. Burton. Neither throws light on any important question. He entered the University of Edinburgh in 1723, and desired to be a Stoic. What his precise course there was is not known. He had a great passion for literature. He mentions certain papers which he intended to publish; no doubt his philosophy. In a letter written to his physician he gives an account of his going over to scepticism, and he begins by saying he always loved literature and letters. He liked poetry and philosophy. He designed to study law. At one time there seemed to be open to him a new field of thought. But in 1729 all ardor was lost; law appeared sickening to him. He thought this coldness sprang from idleness and laziness of temper, and intended to keep on in the same course till he overcame it. Having become disgusted with the law, he attempted to fortify himself by reflections on death, the devil, and pain; but only to ruin his health. Having read many books on morality, he undertook the improvement of his temper and will, as well as his intellect. He endeavored to be self-righteous and stoical. A perfectly wise man, however, is not self-sufficient. He resolved to choose an active life, a merchant's. He was first with Gilbert Elliot, at Bristol, and afterwards traveled on the continent. He wrote a treatise on "Human Nature" while in France (1739). In it he develops his system of the human mind, now acknowledged by Mill. From this treatise we have—

His Philosophy. Hume begins this 1739. All the perceptions of the human mind resolve themselves into two

classes, impressions and ideas. The difference between them is in the degree of force and vividness with which they strike the mind. Those which enter with much force and violence are impressions, and they are passions, etc. By ideas he means the faint images of impressions, which occur in themselves. But he errs in placing together under impressions our passions with our sensations.

Impressions must imply something to be impressed, and the act of impressing. His very language contradicts him. "I always catch myself," he says, "with a perception." (See *infra.*) But we always have the same evidence that we never perceive a perception without a self as perceiving. Kant unfortunately admitted that mind begins with the impressions of ideas, and must afterwards strain reason to arrive at its conclusions. We can never perceive anything but the perception, but we always observe self as perceiving. Hume was not an advance on Hutcheson.

Order of Ideas.

Memory. By it impressions come forth as they were before. It merely re-produces our ideas. He leaves out the fact that we *recognize* them, as having been before the mind in time past. For imagination the ideas are stronger and more lively.

He has three associating principles or laws:

1. Resemblance.

2. Contiguity in time and place. [These two he gets from Aristotle.]

3. Cause and Effect. This is his own. His "Cause and Effect" is redundant, for according to his principles cause and effect are merely contiguity in time and space.

Complex Ideas. He represents them, with Locke, as consisting of substance, mode, and relation, and are formed from simple ideas.

1. Substance. He shows that we have no idea of substance distinct from qualities, nor the substance mind apart from its operations or perceptions. His view of substance is that given by Locke. A substance with him is "a collection of particular qualities united by imagination." He seems to suit facts to theory. He discards the idea of sub-

stratum. We can as little know the qualities as the substances separately.

2. Modes. He examined them by the doctrine of abstract or general ideas (propounded by Berkeley). "They are merely particular ones annexed to a certain term." But when the singulars are real, the universals are real. He overlooks a very essential attribute.

3. Relations. Next he has a very subtle discussion about space and time. It is from the disposition of visible and tangible objects that we receive our ideas of space. Substance and mode are seen in one concrete act. Time we get from the succession of our ideas. He says we cannot form any idea of a vacuum, and that we can never come to a minimum idea. But neither is space nor our idea of space divisible, for space is continuous; and in the perception of objects we perceive them as occupying space. He wanted to undermine the certainty of mathematics. He maintains that things such as lines and angles are in geometry mere ideas of the mind. He sums up thus: "As long as we confine our speculations to the appearances of objects we are safe; but if we go beyond this in our inquiry, I am afraid we are unsafe in most of our conclusions."

Now, as regards existence and knowledge, he argues that we can never advance a step beyond ourselves. This Hume argues logically in his principles. The result he reached was that as long as we confine our speculation to the appearances of objects, without inquiring into their real character and operations, we can never be embarrassed in any question; but if we inquire beyond the appearances, we land ourselves in scepticism and uncertainty. Hence we cannot get beyond relations.

His relations are seven in number:

1 Resemblance, 2 Identity, 3 Space and Time, 4 Proportion, 5 Degree, 6 Contrariety, 7 Cause and Effect.

He divided these relations into two classes.

1. Into such as depend entirely on our ideas compared together, *e. g.*, resemblance, contrariety, degree and proportion or quantity. These never go beyond the ideas.

2. Those which do not depend on our ideas, or such as may be changed without any change of ideas, *e. g.*, the other four, identity, space and time, cause and effect.

In identity and time and space we can never go beyond what is present. The senses, therefore, can never discover the real existence of objects. He holds that we know nothing of the relation of cause and effect. The belief in the existence of an object gives no new ideas besides those involved in our idea of an object. He finds it difficult to explain the nature of belief. The difference between belief and credulity is only vividness of the idea. But our imaginations are often brighter than our memories. He makes this difference to consist solely in its lying in thought. A person who has lost an arm tries long to serve himself with it. He employs this theory to explain our belief in the nature of cause and effect; the one having always been with the other in experience, the effect gives a vivid idea of the cause. This is his explanation of what is implied in power. "Ideas of cause and effect are derived from experience presented in such relation that we cannot help but perceive a lively idea of it."

His definition of cause. An object present and contiguous to another, and so united with it, that the idea of the one determines the mind to form the idea of the other; and the impression of the one to form more lively ideas of the other. He views causation in two lights, Objective and Subjective. Objectively it is mere invariable succession of impression, as *e. g.*, a lighted match and the burning wood. Subjectively he makes it a mere expectation caused by custom.

He dwells on secondary qualities. He does not believe that we perceive our inner, bodily frame. Why have we coherence of impressions? Thought slides from one impression to another, and we mistake the series for a single one. Mind is but a collection of different impressions, connected by relations, but not endowed with unity.

Unfortunately the opponents of Hume have not always met him on right grounds and proper points. They have allowed that we have no idea of power. Causation is not to be regarded as a connection between cause and effect; but a power in substance (the cause) itself to produce the effect.

Two reasons for dwelling on Hume are, that—

All later speculations must proceed from where he left, and that in the reaction against Idealism many have returned to Hume. Huxley says that he followed not Comte but Hume.

Hume said he was prepared to discuss the question why we attribute continued existence to an object, though it is absent from our senses. He shows that the senses give us only present perceptions, and rejects the notion that we can immediately perceive our bodily frame. The thought, according to laws of association, slides from one perception to another. "Mind is but a collection of different impressions, united together by certain relations." We cannot argue from our perceptions to the reality of objects themselves. There is then an antagonism betweén reason and the senses. Reid opposed him, by showing that sensation led us intuitively to believe in an external thing, and the states of mind lead to self. It is better to say we know the external object directly, and are conscious of self in a certain state. According to Hume all arguments for the soul's immortality are extinguished, and the identity we ascribe to mind is merely fictitious. His theory of causation undermines the formation of natural religion. We can answer him by saying that an effect implies a cause. Kant deprived himself of this argument. Hume would make us seek a cause for the Divine Being; but our intuitive convictions will lead us to seek for a cause only of a new event or change.

In the second part of his works he treats of the passions. In book third he treats of morals; and here he starts his utilitarian theory, which is better developed in his "Inquiry Concerning the Principles of Morals." In his moral theory he tries to show that we cannot distinguish between good and evil by reason alone. On the contrary, we may maintain that the mind has the power of disarming good and evil analogous to reason. He sometimes seems to make man a selfish being; again a benevolent one. He makes virtue a good, because beneficial to ourselves. He seems to adhere to the theory of Shaftesbury and Hutcheson as regards the moral sense. By reason he means the discovery of truth and falsehood.

In what does virtue consist? Virtue, he says, consists in the agreeable and the useful. It is distinguished by the pleasure, and vice by the pain that any act gives us. He will not admit that any inanimate object can be virtuous. He never accounts for the sense of obligation. He makes justice good only from its beneficial tendencies. The obligation of keeping a promise is grounded in its utility. But why is there that feeling of condemnation when we neglect such promises?

The practical morality of Hume excludes all higher virtues. There is no repentance. His view of the marriage relation is loose; and he argues that a man may take away his life when it is no longer useful. He says, virtue's "dismal dress thus falls off." What is the conclusion he wishes to gain?

Sometimes we think he wants to lead thinkers to attempt a new method in philosophy. His reasons were to furnish hints to these. In reality, according to him, no certainty can be attained in speculation, and the body of mankind need not trouble themselves about it. British Comtism approaches this, thinking it a satisfactory state of things, when men see they cannot gain any further truth with certainty.

Hume closes: "We find understanding entirely subverts itself, and leaves no certainty for us, even in common life." What injury can a man do by his speculations? A time will come when such studies will be used only as a gymnasium for the mind. He was pleased with men who were moderate in religion, and rather shrunk from avowed atheism.

How is the scepticism of Hume to be met?

1. It must be firmly maintained that an honest man can attain such truth, secular, moral and religious, as is essential to his peace and comfort. Thus we reach the existence of a God and the accountability of man.

2. He who undermines this truth, spontaneously discovered, is doing an injury to mankind, not merely in every-day matters, but in higher concerns. Only a wretched sophistry can lead him to regret the relations between cause and effect. Hume once wondered why a certain

banker's clerk ran away with an amount of money. He was told that it was from reading his essay.

3. The philosopher must inquire into the nature of fundamental truth, and unfold facts by which this is discovered. He must clear up the differences in which the discussion of the questions is involved, and show that the principles are right, though the discussion of them may lead us into danger. Reid believed Berkeley until Hume came, and by Hume Kant was aroused from his dogmatic slumbers. The Scottish school has been occupied in repelling Hume. His assaults may be repelled either at his fundamental principles or afterwards when he has made certain advances. His fundamental principle is that the mind has only impressions and ideas. It must have, also, convictions. Further, he asserts that mind can gather truth only from experience. It has, also, laws. Reid has met him at both points—

a. By making a careful inquiry with the senses, intuitions and consciousness.

b. By establishing that the mind has a primitive reason or common sense.

Reid has not thoroughly cleared up these subjects, but he has established enough to refute Hume.

Kant was strong in logical analysis, and Reid in patient observation. The former allowed Hume's first principles and showed that there is an *a priori* furniture in the mind. But this will not guarantee us any objective reality. Thus he brought in scepticism and saved himself by calling it practical reason; but how can it be shown that the practical reason does not deceive? If you once admit Hume's premises his scepticism is bound to follow. Sir William Hamilton sought to combine Kant and Reid. Mill goes over to Humeism and to Comtism.

CHAPTER VII.

THOMAS REID.

Thomas Reid (1710–1796) was born at Strachan, son of a Presbyterian minister; educated at Marischall College. Professor of Moral Philosophy at Aberdeen and at Glasgow. Succeeded Adam Smith. Died at Glasgow, 1796. Works: On philosophy. *a.* "Inquiry into Human Mind on the Principles of Common Sense, 1763–4." In this he shows a knowledge of physiology; shows that common sense is involved in all sense. *b.* "Essay on the Intellectual and Active Powers" 1780. Here he enumerates the intellectual powers, without a very good classification.

He claims originality in two points.

1. In overthrowing the ideal theory of sense perception. At first he was a believer in Berkeley. Berkeley seemed to him to follow out legitimately all philosophy. Berkeley held that things existed only as some minds existed to perceive them, and if there were no mind there will be no matter. Reid followed this until David Hume appeared. The question is, Is the mind percipient of ideas only, or of things also? Reid never met the ideal theory as thoroughly as Hamilton. In perception Reid had three things—

a. An external object.

b. A sensation in the mind.

c. A perception of the thing suggested by the object, *i. e.*, this sensation suggests a belief in the object.

But Hamilton maintains that we know directly the external object. He shows that we have sensation and perception, that they err, and that they are never separated. When he commenced to edit Reid's works, he said he agreed with him; but as he progresses the differences appear.

2. He founded everything on the principles of common sense. This was his special peculiarity. His is called the

"common sense philosophy." He says there is something in the mind intuitively; and he calls it the principle of common sense. Hamilton defends it. In his work he shows that that phrase has been mentioned by all philosophers, in all ages. Reid gets the word from Shaftesbury, who used it in many senses. It probably came through Hutcheson. The phrase is an unfortunate one, in having three meanings.

a. The Aristotelian meaning of "common percepts." The power which combines the percepts *χοινὴ αἴσθησις*. Common and proper percepts are the two forms given by Aristotle.

b. He makes it equivalent to good sense, practical sagacity; that without which man is a fool, and which he can never acquire. "Common sense is the most uncommon." But this is not the meaning in which the phrase is used here.

c. He employed it as the "*communis sensus.*" The aggregate of original principle, those principles of sense common to all men, and which exist always in the mind.

This is the philosophical sense. Reid used it ambiguously, sometimes in one sense, sometimes in another.

He says reason has two degrees—

1. In which it perceives truth at once—common sense.

2. In which it perceives truth by a process—reasoning.

He divides the principles of common sense into two kinds (two kinds of truth).

1. Those relating to contingent truth.

a. That the senses do not deceive us.

b. That I exist, and am not a mere idea. The thoughts of which I am conscious are the thoughts of the Ego.

c. That I am same to-day as yesterday. What I remember has really happened.

d. Certain expressions of countenance and gestures indicate states of the mind.

2. Those relating to necessary truth. Besides mathematical, grammatical and logical axioms there are metaphysical axioms.

a. Existence of property or quality implies the substance, extension requires an extended object.

b. Contrivance argues a contriver.

c. Design and intelligence in effect imply same in cause.

He has an arrangement of faculties. He treats both of the intellectual and motive powers. He calls the latter the "Active Powers," which is a very unhappy phrase, since both are active.

Estimate of Reid as Philosopher.

A—Excellencies.

1. He follows the inductive method. Locke follows it so far, but does not profess it. He starts from the preconceived theory that all ideas come from two sources. He does not propose to follow induction. Reid professes it, and gives, as an instrument, consciousness.

2. He began with the careful observation of the senses. He takes up the senses one by one to show that they are inlets of knowledge. He shows this on the principle of common sense. Locke made a careful inquiry into the human mind, but did not take much notice of the senses. Reid then proceeded on the inductive method, by starting with the material given by the senses. This was the way of teaching at Glasgow. He was well acquainted with the philosophy of his day. Many metaphysicians, especially Germans, as Fichte, Hegel and others, have done this until the materialistic reaction within the last few years, introducing a physiological psychology.

3. The exclusion of the ideal theory of sense perception. He and Dugald Stewart have shown that Locke held this. He has deserved and taken credit for it. He started out as an Idealist; but later, besides developing the principle of common sense in opposition to Hume, he undermined the Ideal theory, by demonstrating that in sense perception we have (*a*) affection of the organism, (*b*) sensation, and (*c*) perception proper. He says that sensation suggests the perception. This view reminds us of Berkeley.

4. The development of the principles of common sense against Hume. Here we should notice the Aberdeen branch of Scotch philosophy, Beattie and Campbell.

5. Valuable and original remarks on many topics.

Reid and Hamilton should be studied together.

B—Defects.

1. He shows a great want of power of logical analysis, where he has been supplemented by Sir William Hamilton.

2. Hence arises a multiplication of first principles which might have been reduced. His tests are not clearly enunciated.

3. He did not bring out a distinction between what is native and what is necessary; *e. g.*, the discerning of distance by the eye is native, not necessary.

4. There are occasional inconsistencies and incongruities in his writings; *e. g.*, he says sensation suggests perception.

5. The phrase "common sense" is unhappy. Reid's seeming appeal from the subtlety of philosophy to the common sense of the vulgar has gained him the accusation of appealing to prejudice.

DUGALD STEWART. He was born at Edinburgh, 1753, and was educated at Edinburgh University. Thence he went to Glasgow and became pupil of Reid. There was a "blending of harmonies" in him—something Roman in his style. Reid seems to have determined his whole course. He studied Locke very carefully, but was kept from other text books.

1. His dissertation on Philosophy is the work on which his fame chiefly rests. His criticisms are just and mild.

2. In his Elements of the Human Mind, he goes over all the powers of the human mind and classifies them; he begins with the senses and goes through reason, etc.

He is defective in logical grasp, but excels in the concrete. He abounds with middle axioms, which Bacon made the best of all. His influence was great, both in Britain and in France. He contradicted some of Voltaire's evil influences. He was a modest instructor, and had more distinguished pupils than any other man. He was somewhat feeble in health, about middle size, and had dusky eyebrows. He was a very fine reader, and was calm and gentlemanly in manner.

His lectures are made up of detached heads. He endeavors to conceal his originality. The peculiarities of his views are not many. He called principles of common sense "fundamental laws of the human belief or mind," to which we must always come back in our investigations.

[illegible] 28.

[illegible]

[illegible]

aussi [illegible]

Caen [illegible] intention [illegible] grand

[illegible]

conséquent et grand [illegible]

CHAPTER VIII.

GODFREY WILLIAM DE LEIBNITZ.

Godfrey William de Leibnitz. He was born at Leipsic, 1648. His father, a professor in the University, died shortly after his birth. His mother gave him a good education at Leipsic and Jena. He returned to his native city to read law. In his travels through France and England he met Baron de Bohneburg, who favored and promoted his interests. He went to Paris, and there distinguished himself at mathematics. Finally settled in Holland, and became a favorite with the Duke of Hanover, who made him a councillor. He was miserly, and curried favor with the great. He never married, concluding that "marriage was a good thing, but that a wise man should consider it all his life." He died, much regretted, 1716. Frederick of Brandenburg, later Frederick I. of Prussia, founded the Academy of Sciences at Berlin, at the request of Leibnitz.

Works.

He has left no complete system of philosophy in any work. The only important ones (for size) being:

1. Reply to Locke in French, arguing against Locke's Essays, chapter by chapter. Locke died before it was finished, and so Leibnitz thought it unjust to have it published. Appeared after his death, 1761.
2. Theodicea.

View of His Philosophy.

Wolff has tried to systematize it, but he omitted much. Leibnitz opposed the sensationalism then arising. He modified the old maxim: "*Nihil est in intellectu quod non prius fuerit in sensu,* (over which the Stoics placed the ἡγεμονικόν,) into the "*nihil est in intellectu quod non prius fuerit in sensu nisi intellectus ipse,*" *i. e.*, the intellect itself is a source of ideas.

His theory as to the constitution of matter is that of monads, Democritus' atoms.

I. Monads.

1. They have internal principles of variation. Descartes' essence of matter=Extension, Leibnitz'=δύναμις.

2. Each monad has its own principle of action, principle of individualization.

3. All changes occur within. Each monad is a microcosm.

4. Multiplicity in unity.

Monads are:

a. Conscious, composing mind and thought.

b. Unconscious, composing matter.

c. Intermediate, such as have a confused consciousness, (hence Hamilton's theory of unconscious mental cerebration.)

II. Perception.

Rational perception is linked by two laws.

1. Law of Sufficient Reason, which assumes two forms.

a. Subjective: everything conditioned has condition, cause, premise.

b. Objective: principle of cause and effect.

2. Law of Contradiction, in three forms.

a. Self evidence.

b. Contradiction.

c. Excluded middle.

Kant rectified this statement by showing *a priori* truths not under this law. Synthetic judgments not *a priori.*

Tests of Primitive Truth.

Locke—Self-evidence.

Descartes—Clearness and distinction.

Leibnitz—Necessity.

Kant—Necessity and universality.

III. His Mundane Theory.

1. Relation of universe to God. Sublime theory of Optimism. God had before him an infinite number of

worlds, and from them selected the one which, upon the whole, is the best one possible.

Theory of Evil; three kinds.

a. Metaphysical evil, negative, that the bird has no intelligence.

b. Physical evil, real evil. Pain is ~~cause of~~ moral evil.

c. Moral evil; explaining the physical evil. Note: Platonic evil arose from limitation of nature or matter.

2. Relation of objects, one to another. Doctrine of the pre-established harmony, which consists in things being so united as to fit into one another without acting upon each other, *e.g.*, two clocks going alike. There is an analogy between this and the workings of Divine power. According to Leibnitz space and time were relations.

Estimate of Leibnitz as a Philosopher.

A. Excellencies.

1. Universality of his powers. He gets a glimpse of law of conservation of energy.

2. Calls attention to necessary truths; gives them too high place, however. He introduced the test of necessity.

3. Activity of matter in place of Descartes' inertness. Was wrong in denying extension.

4. Grand views of connection of universe with God, (Optimism.)

5. Pre-established harmony is good, though he somewhat overlooked causation.

B. Defects.

1. He attempted everything; therefore, –

2. Left no complete philosophy. Wolfe wrought it out.

3. Too much addicted to speculation.

4. He was wrong in supposing mind does not act on matter, and *vice versa*.

5. His atomic or monad theory had thought, but made God a monad. So all men. He carries it too far.

CHAPTER IX.

EMANUEL KANT.

Emanuel Kant was born in Königsberg, 1724. His father was a Celt; his grandfather a Scotchman. He studied theology, mathematics and physics. Never married. Died in 1804. His great work, "Pure Reason," was published in 1781. In 1784 he published another, "Kritik of Practical Reason." He is the author of the Nebular Hypothesis.

1. His method. It was not the professed induction of Bacon, nor the method of Descartes. Kant calls it "The Kritik," the critical. It is the *a priori* method. Pure reason, he says, can criticise itself. He divides the operations of the mind into knowing or cognitive, feeling and desire or will.

His philosophy consists in a criticism of these three.

His aim is to discover the *a priori* elements of the human mind. He calls them *a priori* forms, and proposes to give an inventory of these forms.

He draws a distinction between analytic and synthetic truth.

In analytic there is nothing affirmed that is not contained in the subject; what is in the predicate is in the subject.

In synthetic there is more in the predicate. He says all analytic truth is *a priori*. The possibility of metaphysics depends on the admission of synthetic judgments *a priori*.

Scheme of His Philosophy.

A. *Knowing.*—Kritik of Pure Reason; *a priori* elements are—

1. Senses—Space, external, Time, internal.
2. Understanding—His 4×3 Categories, under which the mind judges everything.

[illegible] reality

[illegible]

[illegible] showing [illegible]

[illegible] lines [illegible]

[illegible] rather + [illegible]

[illegible] points

Quantity.	Unity. Plurality. Universality.
Quality.	Reality. Negation. Limitation.
Relation.	Substance and accident. Causality and dependence. Action and reaction.
Modality.	Possibility and impossibility. Existence and non-existence. Necessity and contingence.

3. Reason pure. Under it are three rules of reasoning—

a. Categorical.
b. Hypothetical.
c. Disjunctive.

He regulates these by three ideas—

a. Substance.
b. Interdependence of phenomena.
c. God.

The three theistic arguments—

a. Ontological argument. Anselm (Descartes.) "The fool hath said in his heart, there is no God." We have a necessary idea of the infinite and perfect; hence it exists. Kant says being is not implied by the idea. McCosh assumes it, when combined with causation and moral good.

b. Cosmological argument.
This argues from the existence of one thing back to another, and so on to the Creator. Kant says this implies objective existence of cause and effect: but for Kant cause and effect was a merely subjective notion; hence the fallacy. For what, then, is the cause of God?

c. Physico-theological argument.
This is the argument from design. Kant refuses to adopt it, because of its objective view of causality. [See "Intuitions" for Antinomies of Kant, with refutation.]

B. *Desire.*—Kritik of Practical Reason.

The speculative reason gives us forms; this gives us command; hence "Categorical Imperative." Deduce three corollaries:

1. Responsibility. There is a law which we must obey.
2. Immortality of the soul. Things here imperfect. Complement of those to come.
3. God. He had formerly arrived at a metaphysical deity without relations to us. He now reaches a real God.

C. *Feeling.*—Kritik of Judgment. Judgment is mediate between pure and practical reasou. There are two forms:

a. Final cause.
b. Æsthetics.

A. *Knowing.* In his Kritik of Pure Reason his object is to discover the *a priori* elements. *A priori* has two meanings—

1. From Aristotle down to Hume the phrase was applied to the procedure from principles to consequent, and from cause to effect, using the word "cause" in a wider and looser sense than in these times

2. Since Hume, *a priori* denotes whatever is supposed to be in the mind prior to experience.

What, then, is the problem of metaphysics? It is, are there any *a priori* synthetic judgments? All analytic judgments are *a priori;* a great many of our synthetic judgments are *a posteriori.* If there can be no *a priori* synthetic judgments, then there can be no metaphysics.

Now, cause and effect is *a priori*, and that is a synthetic judgment.

He now determines the *a priori* elements, and arranges the faculties, aiming to show the *a priori* elements under each.

1. Senses. These are external and internal, corresponding to sensation and reflection, and to our sense-perception and self-consciousness.

What *a priori* elements are there here? Space and Time. These he chooses to call forms. Necessity and universality declare that all things are perceived by the

senses in space. Yet there is nothing in the external world, he says, corresponding to sense. He was wrong in this, and gave rise to scepticism. Now everything must be perceived in space and time, and this space has no form of itself.

Time is internal. We cannot contemplate anything except in time. But it is nothing in itself; it is a form given by the mind. Time and space are infinite. There must, then, be two infinites. But this cannot be; hence there is no reality in them; they have only a subjective existence. Here Idealism comes in.

2. Understanding, looks at things that have been revealed by the senses. It contemplates them under space and time. The categories of the understanding are twelve. He makes all these to exist in the mind itself, and not in the thing. Under these categories he treats of Formal Logic. Logic can be attempted in a two-fold way:

a. Universal or General Logic.

b. A Particular Logic.

He treats of these in an able manner, deriving each synthetic judgment from a corresponding analytical judgment of Formal Logic.

These categories are purely subjective and ideal. We see how the ideal element grows as we proceed. First in the senses, we have the subjective elements of time and space. Now, the mind in forming these into judgments and propositions, supplies another subjective addition in the categories.

3. Reason. This is something higher. By it he means reasoning in the same sense in which we use it. The *a priori* elements in it are three:

a. Substance.

b. Interdependence of phenomena.

c. God.

These are not in the mere sense. He proceeds as a logician, and finds three kinds of reasoning:

a. Categorical reasoning, which gives a substance. When you affirm something in the predicate of the subject that something is substance.

He criticises the doctrine of substance. Hence lands us in a paralogism. There is no answer to this. We cannot prove substance; if we try, we must assume it.

b. Hypothetical reasoning, interdependence of phenomena, one thing depends upon another. The idea underlying this is that all are in interdependence on each other. Here he shows that pure reason lands us in contradictions, *e. g.*, cause and effect. He says we can prove causality on the one side. Now there is also another position, there must be freedom. There must be then, if it be admitted, two contradictories. The true doctrine is that there are two such principles in the mind.

c. Disjunctive reasoning. He shows by separation that there must be a unity. That unity is God, a mere metaphysical deity.

B. *Desire.* In "Kritik of Practical Reason."

By practical reason he meant the moral power of the conscience. This practical reason brings us back to reality. The speculative is only ideal. This practical reason has a rule categorical. It is imperative and binding on all. This rule is: "Act according to rule, which will admit of being applied to all acting being." This categorical imperative is like the conscience, and the sphere of duty is here. It can never fail to apply. Not so with speculative reason.

He derives three corollaries—

1. Freedom. He says that this command implies that there is freedom. The speculative reason shows man to be free and not free. This freedom is from the fact that man is under law; we are responsible agents.

2. Immortality. Man is under law, and this argues the immortality of the soul. It shows a moral law, and that there are rewards and punishments not given here; there must, therefore, according to it, be some hereafter.

3. God. He gets this from the practical reason. Man is free and under law. These facts point to a future state, and so there must be a God. We cannot avoid this conclusion; it is a necessary truth deep in our moral natures.

C. *Feeling.* He next has a "Kritik of the Judgment" mediate between the two former.

Two subjects are here,

1. ~~Theology~~.

2. Æsthetics.

~~The [illegible]~~ act upon
that [illegible] [illegible] [illegible]
god [illegible] [illegible] [illegible]

1 Man is [illegible]

2 [illegible] [illegible] [illegible] [illegible]

But we must confine ourselves to the two former, the Kritik of Knowing, and of Practical Reason. He shows that the knowing powers deceive us, and we cannot trust them.

Many have been influenced by Kant. He has a great influence in Germany. We cannot understand literature there without some knowledge of his subjective elements.

He has influenced theology and poetry. This influence is to be seen in our own country.

Kant has revolutionized logic. Made it the science of the laws of thought, and all his school call it so. They make it subjective, *a priori*. Yet it is well to follow Aristotle in some senses. Kant's judgments have been termed transposed judgments by McCosh.

Reason. By this we give unity to judgment. Kant confuses reason and reasoning.

By idea he means something *a priori*, the form which produces a unity in judgment. Mere ideas.

They have no objective reality; are mere forms of thinking. If we seek to give them any objective existence, we are landed in difficulties.

Estimate of Kant as a Philosopher.

A. Excellencies.

1. He is essentially anti-Lockeian, and one of the first to attempt an exposition of the *a priori* furniture of the mind.

2. He has the merit of distinguishing between analytic and synthetic judgment.

3. Good observations on space and time. There is something mental in the exercise of the senses.

4. Twelve good categories of the understanding, under which the mind judges.

5. Good exposition of the three ideas to which men can rise, derived from the three forms of reason.

6. Famous for his theistic argument, and criticism on it.

7. High views of morality. Categorical imperative = moral faculty. He defended man's moral nature.

B. Defects.

1. Gives too much place to the subjective. Does not deny reality, but makes it subjective. His method is faulty.

2. Gives the internal furniture a formative, not merely a cognitive power.

3. Gives space and time mere forms, subjective existences.

4. Makes the categories merely formative and subjective (Aristotle's objective.)

5. Ideas he derives are elevating, but he gives them no objective reality, as substance, etc.

6. Kritik of the theistic argument not satisfactory (no objective reality to cause and effect.)

7. Introduced an illusory theory, endeavoring to meet Hume, but did not do so.

8. To obviate the deficiency, he introduced a "practical reason," admitting an essential morality; but that may occur.

9. His morality is of a Stoic, self-righteous nature.

[illegible]

[illegible]

[illegible]

5. [illegible]

6. [illegible]

The following analysis is valuable as a survey of

Reason.

- Three ideals corresponding to the three syllogisms under the category of *Relation.*
  - *Categorical*
    - Gives unity of phenomena in a commonground or substratum; hence
      - *Substance*
        - On which is founded the system of Rational Psychology of Descartes. *Cogito; ergo sum.*
          - Shown to rest on *Paralogisms* of the reason, hence false.
  - *Hypothetical*
    - Gives the idea of *interdependence* of phenomena in a *cosmos*; hence the system of
      - *Rational Cosmology.* Shown to be false, as involving—
        - *Four Antinomies*—
          1. World has and has not a beginning in *time* and *space.*
          2. Every composite is and is not composed of *single parts.*
          3. There is and is not freedom *in the universe.*
          4. An absolutely necessary being does and does not exist.
  - *Disjunctive*
    - Gives the idea of the necessary dependence of all things on an absolute *First Cause or God*; hence
      - *Rational Theology.* Supported by three theistic arguments.
        - *Ontological.*—From ideas in mind to existence of God.
          - False, because involves *argumentum in circulo.*
        - *Cosmological.*—From bare actual existence to necessary existence.
          - Invalid, because involves (1) objective causation and (2) recourse to the ontological argument.
        - *Physico-Theological.*—From design to designer.
          - Invalid, because (1) involves objective causation, and (2) recourse to both the Ontological and Cosmological arguments to complete it.

CHAPTER X.

SIR WILLIAM HAMILTON.

Sir William Hamilton, born in Glasgow, 1791. Studied at Glasgow and Oxford. Became barrister in Edinburgh. Opposed phrenology and the high speculative German philosophy. Became professor of logic and metaphysics in the University of Edinburgh in 1836. Died 1856.

Wholesome tone given to his mind by Reid. Edinburgh made him a philosopher; Oxford, a classical scholar. He eagerly took hold of the critical method of Kant. Jacobi influenced him. Set himself in opposition to the sensualism of France. He tried to combine Scotch and German philosophy, but failed.

His Metaphysics.

Vol. I. On philosophy in general, mental philosophy in particular.

Defence of liberal sciences.

Full of sententious maxims—

"It is ever the contest that pleases us, not the victory."

"What man holds of matter is not he—he is not organism but intelligence."

"Wonder is the mother of knowledge."

Division of the faculties; cognitive, emotive, conative.

Cognitive powers.

I. Presentative. { External=sense-perception.
Internal=self-consciousness.

II. Conservative—Memory; mere power of retention.

III. Reproductive; *a.* Without will=suggestion, μνῆσις.
b. With will=reminiscence, ἀνάμνησις. This from Aristotle.

IV. Representative=imagination.

1741 - 15

[illegible]

V. Elaborative=Comparison, Faculty of relations.

VI. Regulative=Reason, Common Sense.

I. Presentative.

Perception. He has dwelt most largely on perception; mind looks immediately on object; without any "*tertium quid.*"

A. Sense-perception; substantively the same as Locke's sensation. Great attention paid to the senses. Criticises Brown; also the great ideal hypothesis, which has three forms:

1. The representative object is not a modification of mind, but extra-mental (physical or hyperphysical.)

2. The representative object is a modification of mind; dependent for its apprehension, not for its existence, on an act of consciousness.

3. The representative object is a modification of mind; non-existent out of consciousness. The idea and its perceptions are identical. Hamilton maintains that our original perceptions are probably of our organism, or objects in immediate contact. Following the organic affection, there is simultaneously a sensation and perception, the one being strong as the other is weak. The process is infinite; without reasoning, we have immediate perception.

OBJECTIONS.—He overlooks numerous intermediate actions of the mind; processes revealed, beyond doubt, by physiology.

ANSWER.—Never thought of disputing the existence of intermediate steps; but when they are accomplished, what do we perceive? Brain cells? No; the object itself, immediately. It is a mental act, no matter how many precedents there may be; and would not be otherwise if process of reasoning were admitted.

B. Self-consciousness. He makes subtile distinction between consciousness and self-consciousness; the former constituting or being co-extensive with all our faculties of knowledge, the latter being more narrow.

II. Conservative.

He discusses condition of ideas when not before consciousness. Mind constantly laying up power, intellectual and moral. (Aristotle hints this in his δύναμις, ἐντελέχεια, ἐνέργεια.) Hamilton maintains that there are acts below consciousness (monads of third order of Leibnitz;) *e. g.*, murmur of the sea is a sum made of parts; and each wave-noise must have made an impression, else we would not perceive the great total of the noises. Thus, also, the concept of a forest is made up of the conception of all the individual leaves, which are below consciousness. The fact is, that mind does not intuitively perceive sea or forest, but merely sound and color; and by reasoning, we get the external cause. "Those acts," he says, "are below consciousness, which truly have escaped our memory."

III. Reproductive.

Here he discusses association of ideas. He thinks Aristotle reduces laws of association to one general law, (he is wrong,) and finds the law of redintegration incidentally in Augustine. Those thoughts suggest each other, which have previously constituted parts of the same entire or total act of cognition. This cannot account for law of similarity.

V. Elaborative.

This phrase is not very fortunate, as there is elaboration in all mental works. As to comparison proper, he maintains that in so far as two objects resemble each other, the knowledge we have of them is identical, and therefore, to us, the same. As to the relations the mind discovers, Hamilton is very narrow.

1. He says that judgment is virtually pronounced in an act of perception of the *non-ego*, or an act of the self-consciousness of the *ego*.

2. The something of which we are conscious, and of which we predicate existence, is two-fold, the *ego* and the *non-ego*.

3. The recognition of the multiplicity of the co-existent or successive phenomena, and the judgment in regard to their resemblance or divisibility.

4. Comparison of the phenomena, with the native notion of substance.

5. Collection of successive phenomena under the native notion of sensation.

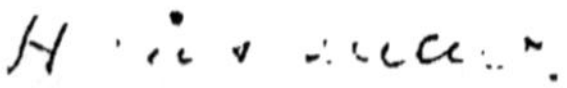

Regulative.

This phrase is good. This must not be taken in the Kantian sense; for, instead of being a separate faculty, the regulative principle consists of laws running through all mental action.

A great defect in his classification of the faculties is his omission of the recognitive power, which saves us from scepticism and agnosticism; cannot get the idea of time by any other faculty.

Philosophy of Relativity, Causation and Infinity.

1. Relativity.

Hamilton holds that the mind does not perceive things as they are, but under modifications and relations imposed by itself. This reminds us of the sophistical "*Homo Mensura.*" He asserts, (1) that existence can be cognized only in special modes; (2) that objects can be known only when they come into certain relations to our faculties; and (3) that these faculties impose modifications upon the object cognized. For example, we will suppose that a cognized object is made up of twelve elements, four contributed by the object, four by the medium through which it is seen, and four by the perceiving mind.

McCosh criticises as follows: He admits (1) that things are known only so far as we have capacities for knowing them; (2) do not know all things or all about anything; our knowledge is partial; (3) the mind perceives objects in relation to its faculties.

He objects (1) To the assertion that we do not know a thing in itself. What we know is the *thing.* The *thing in itself* is a mere abstraction; (2) to the doctrine that mind adds elements of its own, which, he says, lands us in a doctrine of nescience or agnosticism.

2. Causation.

Hamilton's doctrine is that (1) subjective causation, or the causal judgment, is purely negative, being the inability of the mind to conceive either an increase or a diminution of the sum of existence. (2) Objective causation is merely the sum total of all the conditions which constitute a thing. The radical defect of this doctrine is that it leaves out the idea of power, makes the causal judgment positive, not negative.

3. Infinity.

Hamilton divides the realm of existence into two divisions. (1) The conditional, which is the sphere of the relative and the conditioned, and constitutes all possible objects of cognition. (2) The unconditioned, which lies beyond the sphere of the relative and limited. It therefore transcends our powers of thought. In this region of the unconditioned are the Absolute, the Infinite, First Cause, etc.

Now, in accordance with this doctrine, Hamilton holds that the infinite is strictly inconceivable, and that our idea of it is merely our inability to conceive space and time and God as limited. It is, therefore, purely negative. McCosh criticises this. The difficulty lies in the ambiguity of the word conceive. We cannot (1) form a mental *image* of the infinite, nor (2) can we reach it by logical abstraction and generalization. But we can positively think the absence of limits, and this is a positive infinite.

THE END.

www.ingramcontent.com/pod-product-compliance
Lightning Source LLC
Chambersburg PA
CBHW021215270326
41929CB00010B/1144
9783337239152